Writing, Audio & Video Workbook

Needham, Massachusetts
Upper Saddle River, New Jersey

4 5 6 7 8 9 10   05 04

ISBN 0-13-036007-4

Realidades ①

Para empezar

Nombre _____

Hora _____

Fecha _____

AUDIO

Actividad 1

You are at a party with students visiting from Ecuador. You have practiced several responses to the things they might say when you meet them. Listen to each question or statement and write the letter of the best response in the blank. You will hear each statement or question twice.

a. Me llamo ...

b. Muy bien, gracias.

c. Regular.

d. Mucho gusto.

e. Igualmente.

f. Hasta mañana.

1. _____
2. _____
3. _____
4. _____
5. _____
6. _____

Actividad 2

You have lost your dog, so you put up signs in your neighborhood asking your neighbors to call you if they see him. You will hear six messages on your answering machine from neighbors who have seen your dog. You will not understand everything they say, but listen carefully to find out their house number and what time they called so that you can track down your dog. Write down each house number and time on the chart. You will hear each message twice.

	NÚMERO DE CASA (House number)	HORA DE LA LLAMADA (Time of call)
1.	_____	_____
2.	_____	_____
3.	_____	_____
4.	_____	_____
5.	_____	_____
6.	_____	_____

Nombre _____

Hora _____

Fecha _____

AUDIO

Actividad 3

A new student has come into your Spanish class. He seems lost when the teacher asks the students to take out certain items. As you listen to what the teacher says, help him by identifying the picture that matches the item the teacher is asking the students to get out for class. You will hear each command twice.

Modelo   _f_   1. _b_   2. _c_   3. _e_   4. _d_   5. _a_

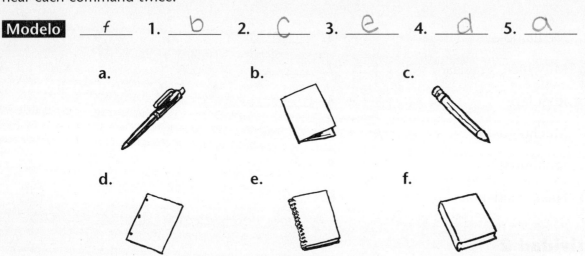

a.

b.

c.

d.

e.

f.

Actividad 4

Your teacher is using a map and an alphabet/number grid to plan a class trip to Spain. The five dots on the grid represent cities in Spain where your group will stop. Listen as you hear the first letter/number combination, as in the game of Bingo. Find that dot on the grid and label it "1." Next to it, write the name of the city. After you hear the second letter/number combination, find the second dot and label it "2," writing the name of the city next to it, and so on for the rest of the dots. Connect the dots to show the route of the class trip. You will hear each phrase twice.

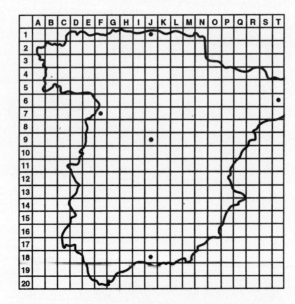

Realidades 1

Para empezar

Nombre _____

Fecha _____

Hora _____

AUDIO

Actividad 5

While on vacation in Uruguay, your teacher visits an elementary school classroom. Each student in the class tells your teacher his or her birthday (**cumpleaños**) and what the weather is like at that time of the year in Uruguay. Remember, in South America the seasons are the reverse of those in the United States. In the first column write out each student's date of birth, and in the second column what season his or her birthday is in. You will hear each sentence twice.

		DATE OF BIRTH	SEASON
1.	Juan	20 de julio	el invierno
2.	María	17 de septiembre	
3.	Miguel	7 de mayo	el otoño
4.	Óscar	19 de deciembre	
5.	Carolina	15 de enero	
6.	Marta	16 de octubre	
7.	Elena	31 de marzo	el
8.	Pedro	25 de junio	el invierno

Realidades 1

Para empezar

Nombre _____

Fecha _____

Hora _____

WRITING

Actividad 6

Describe the monster below, telling how many of each body part he has (**El monstruo tiene ...**). Each blank corresponds to one letter. Each letter corresponds to a number, which appears underneath the blank. Use these numbers to figure out which sentence refers to which body part. The first one has been done for you.

d,a, b,c ,F, e,

Modelo El monstruo tiene D O S   C A B E Z A S .
                              9 15 20 2 10 19 1 3 10 20

1. El monstruo tiene O C h O   O J O S .
                      15 2 8 15 15 17 15 20

2. El monstruo tiene U N A   N A R I Z en cada cabeza.
                      6 22 10 22 10 4 5 3

3. El monstruo tiene U N A   B O C A en cada cabeza. one mouth
                      6 22 10 19 15 2 10

4. El monstruo tiene C U A + R O   B R A Z O S . four arms
                      2 6 10 11 4 15 19 4 10 3 15 20

5. El monstruo tiene + R E S   D E D O S en cada mano. three fingers
                      11 4 1 20 9 1 9 15 20

6. El monstruo tiene S E I S   P I E R N A S . six legs
                      20 1 5 20 16 5 1 4 22 10 20

Actividad 7

A. It is September and school is finally in session. You already have some important dates to mark on the calendar. To make sure you have the right day, write the day of the week that each date falls on.

SEPTIEMBRE						
lunes	martes	miércoles	jueves	viernes	sábado	domingo
		1	2	3	4	5
6	7	8	9	10	11	12
13	14	15	16	17	18	19
20	21	22	23	24	25	26
27	28	29	30			

1. el tres de septiembre _viernes_

2. el veinte de septiembre _lunes_

3. el primero de septiembre _miércoles_

4. el veinticuatro de septiembre _viernes_

5. el doce de septiembre _domingo_

6. el dieciocho de septiembre _sábado_

7. el siete de septiembre _martes_

B. Now, write in what month the following holidays occur.

1. el Día de San Valentín _febrero_

2. el Día de San Patricio _marzo_

3. la Navidad _diciebre_

4. el Año Nuevo _enero_

5. el Día de la Independencia _julio_

Actividad 8

Answer the questions below according to the map.

1. ¿Qué tiempo hace en el norte de México?

   _____

2. ¿Hace buen tiempo en el sur?

   _____

3. ¿Qué tiempo hace en el centro de México?

   _____

4. ¿Hace frío o calor en el oeste?

   _____

5. ¿Qué tiempo hace en el este?

   _____

6. ¿Qué estación es, probablemente?

   _____

Realidades ❶

Capítulo 1A

Nombre _____

Hora _____

Fecha _____

VIDEO

Introducción

Actividad 1

Do you like the video so far? Did you enjoy meeting the characters? Are you curious to find out more about their home cities? Look at the map below. Then, write the names of the video friends that live at each location. As you are doing this exercise, begin to familiarize yourself with the names of these locations: Madrid, España; Ciudad de México, México; San José, Costa Rica; San Antonio, Texas.

| Esteban y Angélica | Ignacio y Ana | Claudia y Teresa | Raúl y Gloria |

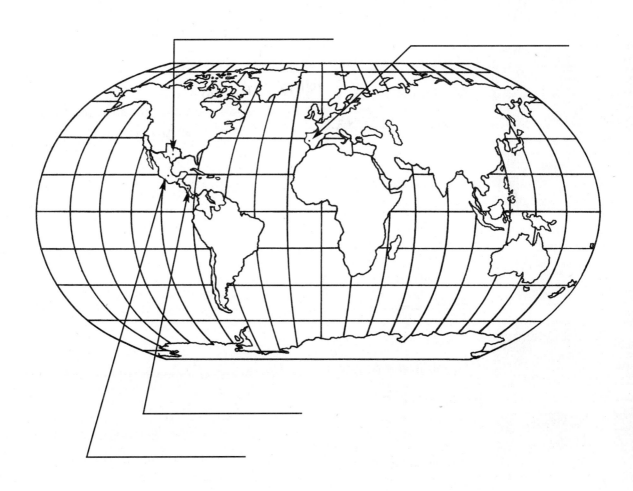

Realidades ➊

Nombre _____

Hora _____

Capítulo 1A

Fecha _____

VIDEO

¿Comprendes?

Actividad 2

Match the characters with the activities they like to do or do not like to do.

1. Me llamo Ignacio y tengo 17 años. _____

a. Me gusta escuchar música también. Pero me gusta más hablar por teléfono.

2. Yo me llamo Ana y tengo 15 años. _____

b. Me gusta usar la computadora.

3. Me llamo Claudia y tengo 16 años. _____

c. A mí me gusta tocar la guitarra.

4. Y yo soy Teresa. Tengo 15 años. _____

d. Me gusta practicar deportes, correr y montar en bicicleta.

5. Soy Esteban. Tengo 15 años. _____

e. Me gusta leer libros y revistas.

6. Yo me llamo Angélica y tengo 16 años. _____

f. A mí me gusta ir a la escuela.

7. Soy Raúl y tengo 15 años. _____

g. Me gusta más jugar videojuegos.

8. Me llamo Gloria y tengo 14 años. _____

h. A mí no me gusta ni correr ni montar en bicicleta. A mí me gusta patinar.

Actividad 3

Decide whether response a, b, or c best describes the characters in each question.

1. When they are outside, what does Ana ask Ignacio? _____
   a. ¿Te gusta hablar por teléfono?
   b. ¿Qué te gusta hacer?
   c. ¿Te gusta tocar la guitarra?

2. Claudia and Teresa live in Mexico. What do they both like to do? _____
   a. pasar tiempo con amigos
   b. jugar videojuegos
   c. usar la computadora

3. What sports do Esteban and Angélica talk about? _____
   a. correr, montar en bicicleta y patinar
   b. esquiar, correr y nadar
   c. jugar al básquetbol, jugar al fútbol y montar en bicicleta

4. Does Raúl like to go to school? _____
   a. Sí. A Raúl le gusta mucho ir a la escuela.
   b. No. No le gusta nada.
   c. Pues… más o menos.

Y, ¿qué más?

Actividad 4

You have just seen and heard what these eight video friends like or do not like to do. Now fill in the blanks below to tell about things that you like to do and do not like to do.

1. Me gusta _____.

2. A mí me gusta más _____.

3. A mí no me gusta _____.

4. A mí no me gusta ni _____.

Actividad 5

You can learn a lot about a person from what he or she likes to do. You will hear two people from each group of three describe themselves. Listen and match the descriptions to the appropriate pictures. Put an *A* underneath the first person described, and a *B* underneath the second person described. You will hear each set of statements twice.

1. Luisa _____ Marta _____ Carmen _____

2. Marco _____ Javier _____ Alejandro _____

3. Mercedes _____ Ana _____ María _____

4. Carlos _____ Jaime _____ Luis _____

5. Isabel _____ Margarita _____ Cristina _____

Actividad 6

A group of students from Peru will visit your school. Since your class will be hosting the students, your teacher is trying to match each of you with a visiting student who likes to do the same things as you do. Listen to the questions and write the students' answers in the blanks. Then, write which of the activities you like better. Find out if the student has the same preferences as you do. Follow the model. You will hear each conversation twice.

Modelo   Guillermo: _____ *cantar* _____

         A mí: _____ *Me gusta más bailar* _____ .

1. Paco: _____

     A mí: _____ .

2. Ana María: _____

     A mí: _____ .

3. José Luis: _____

     A mí: _____ .

4. Maricarmen: _____

     A mí: _____ .

5. Luisa: _____

     A mí: _____ .

AUDIO

Actividad 7

As one of the judges at your school's fall carnival, your job is to mark on the master tic tac toe board the progress of a live tic-tac-toe competition between Team X and Team O.

As each contestant comes to the microphone, you will hear por X or por O to indicate for which team he or she is playing. The contestant has to answer a question about activities in order to claim the square. Listen for the activity mentioned in each question, and put either an *X* or an *O* in the box under the picture of that activity.

At the end of this game round, see which team won! You will hear each statement twice.

Who won the game? _____

Realidades ①

Capítulo 1A

Nombre _____

Fecha _____

Hora _____

AUDIO

Actividad 8

Luisa, the host of your school's radio station talk show, is interviewing four new students. As you listen to the interview, write down one thing that each student likes to do, and one thing that each student does not like to do. You will hear the entire question and answer session repeated. You will hear this conversation twice.

	Armando	Josefina	Carlos	Marta
Likes	jugar videojvegos	tacor la guitarra	leer	nadar y nontar en biclaleta
Dislikes	practicar deparles	escchos musica	nadar en el varana	cequiar patiar

Actividad 9

As you turn on the radio, you hear a Spanish radio D.J. talking about the "Top Ten Tips" for being happy during this school year. As you listen, match the suggestion to one of the pictures and number them in the order the suggestions were given on the air. Remember to listen for cognates!

a. # 7	b. # 9	c. # 3	d. # 8	e. # 2
f. # 10	g. # 6	h. # 5	i. # 1	j. # 4

Realidades 1

Capítulo 1A

Nombre _____

Fecha _____

Hora _____

WRITING

Actividad 10

Students like to do all sorts of activities during their free periods. Look at the picture below and write what each student is saying he or she likes to do. Then say whether or not you like to do those things. Follow the model.

Modelo EL PROFESOR: *A mí me gusta trabajar.*

TÚ: *A mí me gusta trabajar también.*

ESTUDIANTE #1: _____

TÚ: _____

ESTUDIANTE #2: _____

TÚ: _____

ESTUDIANTE #3: _____

TÚ: _____

ESTUDIANTE #4: _____

TÚ: _____

ESTUDIANTE #5: _____

TÚ: _____

ESTUDIANTE #6: _____

TÚ: _____

Realidades 1

Nombre _____

Hora _____

Capítulo 1A

Fecha _____

WRITING

Actividad 11

It is your first day at your new school, and your new friend Elena is interviewing you for the school newspaper. In the spaces provided, write your answers to the questions that Elena asks you.

ELENA: —Buenos días. ¿Cómo estás?

TÚ: —_____

ELENA: —¿Qué te gusta hacer?

TÚ: —_____

ELENA: —¿Te gusta ir a la escuela?

TÚ: —_____

ELENA: —¿Qué te gusta hacer en casa?

TÚ: —_____

ELENA: —¿Te gusta escribir o leer cuentos?

TÚ: —_____

ELENA: —¿Qué más te gusta hacer?

TÚ: —_____

ELENA: —Pues, muchas gracias por la entrevista. Buena suerte.

TÚ: —_____

Realidades 1

Capítulo 1A

Nombre _____

Hora _____

Fecha _____

WRITING

Actividad 12

A. Your classmates have signed up for different clubs. Look at the flyers below to see who signed up for which club. Then, decide how each student might answer the questions below based on the club that each one signed up for.

El Club Educativo	El Club Deportista	EL CLUB MUSICAL
El club ideal para estudiantes a quienes les gusta ir a la escuela.	El club ideal para estudiantes a quienes les gusta practicar deportes.	El club ideal para estudiantes a quienes les gusta la música.
Actividades:	Actividades:	**ACTIVIDADES:**
• usar la computadora • leer y escribir cuentos • estudiar	• nadar • correr • practicar deportes	• TOCAR EL PIANO O LA GUITARRA • CANTAR • BAILAR
Eduardo _____ Eugenia _____ Esteban _____	Diana _____ Dolores _____ Diego _____	MARICARMEN _____ MANOLO _____ MÓNICA _____

Modelo   Eduardo, ¿te gusta tocar la guitarra?

No, no me gusta tocar la guitarra. Me gusta estudiar.

1. Diana, ¿te gusta leer o escribir cuentos?

_____

2. Manolo, ¿qué te gusta hacer?

_____

3. Diego, ¿te gusta ir a la escuela para usar la computadora?

_____

4. Mónica, ¿te gusta nadar o correr?

_____

5. Eugenia, ¿qué te gusta hacer?

_____

B. Now, pick which club you would join and say why. Follow the model.

Modelo   *Prefiero el Club Educativo porque me gusta ir a la escuela.*

Prefiero el Club _____ porque _____

_____

Actividad 13

A. Write two sentences about things that you like to do, and two sentences about things that you do not like to do. Follow the model.

Modelo *A mí me gusta leer.* _____

No me gusta correr. _____

1. _____

2. _____

3. _____

4. _____

B. Now, use your sentences from Part A to write a letter to your new penpal that will tell her a little bit about you.

29/9/2003

Saludos,

_____

_____

_____

_____

_____

También _____

_____

_____

_____

Un abrazo,

_____

Antes de ver el video

Actividad 1

During the video, Teresa, Claudia, Pedro, and Esteban describe each other in e-mails. How would you describe yourself? Below is a list of descriptive words. Check off the words that describe you.

Soy...

- ☑ artístico, -a
- ☐ atrevido, -a
- ☐ deportista
- ☐ desordenado, -a
- ☐ estudioso, -a
- ☑ gracioso, -a

- ☐ impaciente
- ☑ inteligente
- ☐ ordenado, -a
- ☐ paciente
- ☐ reservado, -a
- ☐ serio, -a

- ☐ simpático, -a
- ☑ sociable
- ☐ talentoso, -a
- ☐ trabajador, -ora

¿Comprendes?

Actividad 2

Fill in the blanks with the appropriate word or phrase from the bank. You may have to watch the video several times to remember each character well.

misteriosa	reservado	ordenados	inteligente
serio	trabajadora	sociable	
simpática	hablar por teléfono	buena	

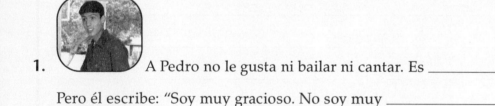

1. A Pedro no le gusta ni bailar ni cantar. Es _____.

Pero él escribe: "Soy muy gracioso. No soy muy _____."

Nombre _____   Hora _____

Fecha _____

VIDEO

2. Teresa, desde un cibercafé en la Ciudad de México, escribe: "Yo soy *Chica*

_____."

3. Ella es la _____ amiga de Claudia.

4. Le gusta _____ , pero no le gusta ir a la escuela.

5. En la computadora, Claudia se llama *Chica* _____ .

6. A ella le gusta la escuela; es muy _____ , estudiosa

y _____ .

7. También le gustan los chicos inteligentes y _____ .

8. A Pedro le gusta *Chica misteriosa.* Ella también es una chica _____ .

Actividad 3

According to Esteban, Pedro is quiet and reserved. Yet, in his e-mail, he writes the opposite. Read what he writes about himself in his e-mail. Then, write what he is really like by filling in the blanks.

> Me llamo Chico sociable. ¡Qué coincidencia! Me gusta pasar tiempo con mis amigos... Me gusta escuchar música. Según mis amigos soy muy gracioso. No soy muy serio. Escríbeme.

1. *Chico sociable,* el _____ de Esteban, se llama _____ .

2. Según Esteban, él no es un chico _____ . Él es _____ .

3. A Pedro no le gusta ni _____ ni _____ .

4. Pedro no es muy _____ . Él es muy _____ .

Y, ¿qué más?

Actividad 4

Describe people you know using each of the adjectives from the following list. Follow the model.

paciente	inteligente	sociable	impaciente	deportista

Modelo   *La profesora de español es muy inteligente.*

_____

_____

_____

_____

Nombre _____   Hora _____

Fecha _____   **AUDIO**

Actividad 5

You are a volunteer for a service at your school that helps new students meet other new students in order to make the transition easier. People who are interested in participating in this program have left messages describing themselves. Listen as the students describe themselves, and put a check mark in at least two columns that match what each student says. Then write the names of the most well-matched students. You will hear each statement twice.

BUENOS AMIGOS

	CARMEN	PABLO	ANA	ANDRÉS	RAQUEL	JORGE
serio(a)						
reservado(a)						
deportista						
estudioso(a)						
talentoso(a)						
gracioso(a)						
atrevido(a)						
trabajador(a)						
artístico(a)						
sociable						
romántico(a)						

BUENOS AMIGOS:

1. _____ y _____

2. _____ y _____

3. _____ y _____

Actividad 6

What is your favorite season of the year? Your choice could say a lot about you. Listen as talk-show psychologist Doctor Armando describes people according to their preferred season (**estación preferida**) of the year. What characteristics go with each season? Listen and put a check mark in the appropriate boxes. By the way, is it true what he says about you and your favorite season? You will hear each statement twice.

Mi estación preferida es _____. Según el Dr. Armando, yo soy

_____.

Realidades ①

Capítulo 1B

Nombre _____

Hora _____

Fecha _____

AUDIO

Actividad 7

Your Spanish teacher encourages you to speak Spanish outside of class. As you walk down the hall, you hear parts of your classmates' conversations in Spanish. Listen to the conversations and decide whether they are talking about a boy, a girl, or if you can't tell by what is being said. Place a check mark in the appropriate box of the table. You will hear each statement twice.

	#1	#2	#3	#4	#5	#6	#7	#8
(boy)				✓	✓		✓	
(girl)	✓	✓				✓		✓
?			✓					✓

Actividad 8

Listen as Nacho describes his ex-girlfriend. How many things do they have in common? Put an X on the pictures that show ways in which they are very different and put a circle around the pictures that show ways they are very similar. You will hear each set of statements twice.

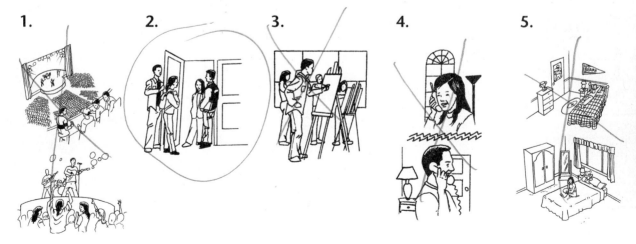

1.   2.   3.   4.   5.

Realidades ❶

Capítulo 1B

Nombre _____

Hora _____

Fecha _____

AUDIO

Actividad 9

Some people say we are what we dream! Listen as Antonieta calls in and describes her dream (**sueño**) to Doctor Armando, the radio talk show psychologist. Draw a circle around the pictures below that match what she dreams about herself.

After you hear Antonieta's call, tell a partner what kinds of things would be in a dream that reveals what you like to do and what kind of person you are. You might begin with "**En mi sueño, me gusta...**". You will hear this dialogue twice.

Realidades 1

Capítulo 1B

Nombre _____

Hora _____

Fecha _____

WRITING

Actividad 10

A. Fill in the words using the art as clues.

1. Marta es una chica _____.

2. Cristina es mi amiga _____.

3. Alicia es muy _____.

4. Isa es una chica _____.

5. Alejandro es muy _____.

6. Carlos es un chico _____.

7. Kiko es _____.

8. Pepe es mi amigo _____.

B. Now, check your answers by finding them in the word search.

```
N E P M V P I Q U U T D
T R A B A J A D O R A E
A S O I D U T S E D G S
L A K U X M A L E A R O
E M D I C Z P P O C A R
N T P A O X O J Z I C D
T I U M N R U F R T I E
O Q K I T E I T E S O N
S M X I E T D G P I S A
A O S L U R M R Y T O D
P T L A E U U J O R H O
A S O C I A B L E A E T
```

Realidades 1

Capítulo 1B

Nombre _____

Hora _____

Fecha _____

WRITING

Actividad 11

Frida and Diego, who are opposites, are talking on the phone. Frida, the sociable one, is doing all the talking. Using the pictures of the friends below, write what Frida might be saying about herself and about Diego. Follow the models.

Modelo	*Yo soy deportista.*	Modelo	*Tú eres paciente.*

1. _____   **1.** _____

2. _____   **2.** _____

3. _____   **3.** _____

4. _____   **4.** _____

5. _____   **5.** _____

Actividad 12

Answer the following questions. Be sure to use the definite or indefinite article where appropriate. Follow the model.

> **Modelo**   ¿Cómo es tu mamá (*mother*)?
>
> *Ella es simpática y graciosa.*

1. ¿Cómo eres tú?

   _____

2. ¿Cómo es tu profesor(a) de español?

   _____

3. ¿Cómo es tu mejor amigo(a)?

   _____

4. ¿Cómo es el presidente?

   _____

5. ¿Cómo es el director/la directora (*principal*) de tu escuela?

   _____

6. ¿Qué te duele?

   _____

7. ¿Cuál es la fecha de hoy?

   _____

8. ¿Cuál es la fecha del Día de la Independencia?

   _____

9. ¿Cuál es tu estación favorita?

   _____

10. ¿Qué hora es?

   _____

Nombre _____

Hora _____

Fecha _____

WRITING

Actividad 13

A reporter for the school newspaper has asked you and several other students in your classroom to submit an article for the paper. The article is about personality traits and activities people like and dislike.

A. Think about your own personality traits. Write four adjectives that describe what you are like and four that describe what you are not like.

SOY

Soy gracioso

Soy perezosa

Soy impacite

Soy atrevido

NO SOY

No soy estudioso

No soy paciente

No soy antipático

No soy serio

B. Now, write four things that you like to do and four things that you do not like to do.

ME GUSTA

Me gusta bailar

Me gusta cantar

Me gusta correr

Me gusta escuchar música

NO ME GUSTA

No me gusta equiar

No me gusta patinar

No me gusta trabajar

No me gusta tocarla guitarra

C. Now, write your article using the information you have compiled about yourself.

_____
_____
_____
_____
_____
_____
_____
_____
_____

Antes de ver el video

Actividad 1

Think of two of your favorite and two of your least favorite classes. Write the name of each class, when you have it, and why it is your favorite or least favorite.

Clase	Hora	Comentarios

¿Comprendes?

Actividad 2

Claudia had a bad day. Circle the correct answer to explain what happened to her.

1. Claudia tiene un día difícil en el colegio (*high school*). ¿Por qué?
   a. A Claudia no le gusta su colegio.
   b. Claudia no tiene amigos.
   c. Tiene problemas con el horario.
   d. A Claudia no le gustan las matemáticas.

2. ¿En qué hora tiene Claudia la clase de matemáticas?
   a. en la primera hora
   b. en la tercera hora
   c. en la quinta hora
   d. todas las anteriores (*all of the above*)

3. Claudia habla con la persona que hace el horario. ¿Cómo se llama?
   a. Sra. Santoro   b. Sr. López   c. Srta. García   d. Sr. Treviño

4. Para Teresa la clase de inglés es
   a. aburrida.   b. interesante.   c. fantástica.   d. difícil.

5. En la tercera hora Claudia piensa que las matemáticas son aburridas, porque
   a. es el primer día de clases.
   b. la profesora es muy divertida.
   c. tiene seis clases de matemáticas hoy.
   d. no entiende las matemáticas.

Realidades ①

Capítulo 2A

Nombre

Hora

Fecha

VIDEO

Actividad 3

Write **cierto** (*true*) or **falso** (*false*) next to each statement.

1. La clase de matemáticas es muy fácil para Claudia. _____

2. Teresa habla con el Sr. Treviño del problema con su horario. _____

3. Teresa y Claudia tienen el almuerzo a la misma hora. _____

4. Teresa tiene la clase de ciencias sociales en la tercera hora. _____

Y, ¿qué más?

Actividad 4

Complete the paragraph with information about your teachers, classes, school, and friends.

El profesor / La profesora que más me gusta es el Sr. / la Sra. _____.

Él / Ella enseña la clase de _____ en la _____ hora y su clase

es muy _____ .

Después de la _____ hora tengo el almuerzo. Me gusta mucho porque

puedo estar con _____ y _____ ; ellos / ellas son mis

amigos / amigas.

El director / La directora de mi colegio se llama _____. Él / Ella es muy

_____ y _____ .

Actividad 5

You overhear several people in the hall trying to find out if they have classes together this year. As you listen to each conversation, write an *X* in the box under *Sí* if they have a class together, or under *NO* if they do not. You will hear each conversation twice.

	SÍ	NO
1.	_____	_____
2.	_____	_____
3.	_____	_____
4.	_____	_____
5.	_____	_____

Actividad 6

As you stand outside the school counselor's office, you hear four students trying to talk to him. They are all requesting to get out of a certain class. From the part of the conversation that you hear, write in the blank the class from which each student is requesting a transfer. You will hear each statement twice.

	CLASE	PROFESOR(A)
1.	matemáticas	el profesor Pérez
2.	arte	la profesora Muñoz
3.	español	el profesor Cortez
4.	ciencias sociales	la profesora Lenis
5.	almuerzo	
6.	ciencias	el profesor Gala
7.	educación física	el profesor Fernández
8.	inglés	la profesora Ochoa

1. La clase de _____

2. La clase de _____

3. La clase de _____

4. La clase de _____

© Pearson Education, Inc. All rights reserved.

AUDIO

Actividad 7

Emilio, a new student from Bolivia, is attending his first pep assembly! He is eager to make friends and begins talking to Diana, who is sitting next to him. Listen to their conversation. If they have something in common, place a check mark in the column labeled **Ellos**. If the statement only applies to Emilio, place a check mark in the column labeled **Él**. If the statement only applies to Diana, place a check mark in the column labeled **Ella**. **Note:** Be sure you have placed a check mark in ONLY one of the columns for each statement. You will hear the conversation twice.

INFORMACIÓN	ÉL	ELLA	ELLOS
Tiene la clase de español en la primera hora.	✓		
Tiene la clase de español en la segunda hora.		✓	
Tiene una profesora simpática.		✓	
Tiene una profesora graciosa.	✓		
Tiene una clase de arte en la quinta hora.		✓	
Tiene una clase de educación física en la quinta hora.			
Practica deportes.			✓
Estudia mucho en la clase de matemáticas.			✓
Es trabajador(a).			
Tiene mucha tarea.	✓		
Tiene almuerzo a las once y media.			

AUDIO

Actividad 8

Listen as four people talk about what they do during the day. There will be some things that all four people do and other things that not all of them do. Fill in the grid with a check mark if the person says he or she does a certain activity. Also, fill in the **Yo** column with a check mark for the activities that you do every day. You will hear each set of statements twice.

	EVA	DAVID	RAQUEL	JOSÉ	YO
(reading by lamp)	✓	✓			
(computer)	✓	✓	✓	✓	
(talking/window)		✓	✓	✓	
(bicycle)			✓		
(painting)		✓			
(basketball)	✓	✓	✓		
(radio/boombox)	✓			✓	

Actividad 9

You and your family are considering hosting a student from Costa Rica for a semester. Before you make the decision, you want to know a little about the student. Listen to part of a recording that the students from Costa Rica made for your class. Use the grid to keep track of what each of the students says. You will then use this information to decide which student would be the most compatible for you and your family. You will hear each set of statements twice.

Estudiante	Característica(s) de la personalidad	Clase favorita	Actividades favoritas
JORGE			
LUZ			
MARCO			
CRISTINA			

Which student is most like you? _____

Nombre _____ Hora _____

Fecha _____

WRITING

Actividad 10

Your classmates are curious about your schedule at school. Using complete sentences, tell them what classes you have during the day. Follow the model.

Modelo *Yo tengo la clase de inglés en la segunda hora.* _____

1. _____

2. _____

3. _____

4. _____

5. _____

6. _____

7. _____

Actividad 11

Answer the following questions using the subject pronoun suggested by the pictures. Follow the model.

¿Quiénes usan la computadora?

Modelo *Ellos usan la computadora.* _____ .

¿Quién habla con Teresa?

1. _ella habla con teresa_ .

¿Quién habla con Paco?

2. _ello habla con paco_ .

Writing Activities — *Capítulo 2A* **35**

Nombre _____

Hora _____

Fecha _____

WRITING

3. ¿Quiénes hablan?

_____ .

4. ¿Cómo es el Sr. García?

_____ .

5. Ana, ¿tienes la clase de arte en la primera hora?

Sí, _____ .

Ana

6. ¿Cristina y yo somos muy buenas amigas?

Sí, _____ .

Cristina   Yo

Nombre _____ Hora _____

Fecha _____ **WRITING**

Actividad 12

A new student at your school has come to you for information about how things work at your school and what your day is like. Answer the student's questions truthfully in complete sentences. Follow the model.

Modelo ¿La secretaria habla mucho por teléfono?

Sí, ella habla mucho _____.

1. ¿Estudias inglés en la primera hora?

   _____.

2. ¿Quién enseña la clase de matemáticas?

   _____.

3. ¿Necesito un diccionario para la clase de arte?

   _____.

4. ¿Cantas en el coro (*choir*)?

   _____.

5. ¿Pasas mucho tiempo en la cafetería?

   _____.

6. ¿Uds. practican deportes en la clase de educación física?

   _____.

7. ¿Los estudiantes usan las computadoras en la clase de ciencias naturales?

   _____.

8. ¿Uds. bailan en la clase de español?

   _____.

9. ¿Los profesores tocan el piano en la clase de música?

   _____.

10. ¿Los estudiantes hablan mucho en la clase de francés?

    _____.

Actividad 13

A. List two classes that you have, when you have them, and who the teacher is.

Clase	Hora	Profesor(a)
1. _español_	_primero la clase_	_Sr. Dorado_
2. _matemáticas_	_segundo la clase_	_Sr. Haun_

B. Now, write complete sentences about whether or not you like each class from Part A. Make sure to tell why you do or do not like each class.

Clase 1: _____

_____

_____

_____

Clase 2: _____

_____

_____

_____

C. Now, using the information from Parts A and B, write a paragraph about one of the classes. Make sure to tell the name of the class, when you have it, and who the teacher is. You should also describe your teacher, tell what you do in class, and say whether or not you like the class.

_____

_____

_____

_____

_____

_____

_____

Antes de ver el video

Actividad 1

Look around your classroom and make a list of five items that you see. Then, describe their location. Follow the model.

COSA	DÓNDE ESTÁ
Modelo *la papelera*	*debajo del reloj*
1. _____	_____
2. _____	_____
3. _____	_____
4. _____	_____
5. _____	_____

¿Comprendes?

Actividad 2

Using the screen grabs as clues, answer the following questions with the correct information from the video.

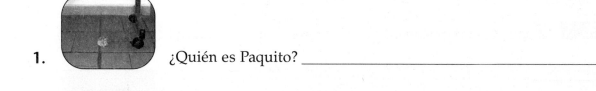

1. ¿Quién es Paquito? _____

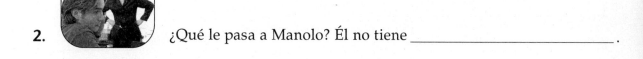

2. ¿Qué le pasa a Manolo? Él no tiene _____.

3. ¿Quién tiene el hámster? _____

4. Los estudiantes están en _____.

5. ¿Para qué es el hámster? Es para _____.

Actividad 3

Next to each phrase, write the name of the character who said it in the video.

1. "¿Un ratón en la clase de ciencias sociales? ¡Imposible!" _____

2. "¡No es un ratón! Es mi hámster." _____

3. "Señorita, necesito hablar con usted más tarde." _____

4. "Carlos, no tengo mi tarea." _____

5. "¡Aquí está! Está en mi mochila." _____

6. "Paquito, mi precioso. Ven aquí. ¿Estás bien?" _____

Y, ¿qué más?

Actividad 4

Imagine that Paquito is running around in your classroom. Using the prepositions that you have just learned, indicate four places where he might be. Follow the example below.

Modelo *Paquito está encima de la mochila.*

1. _____

2. _____

3. _____

4. _____

Realidades ❶

Capítulo 2B

Nombre _____ Hora _____

Fecha _____

AUDIO

Actividad 5

As you look at the picture, decide whether the statements you hear are **ciertos** or **falsos**. You will hear each statement twice.

1. cierto falso		**6.** cierto falso		**11.** cierto falso	
2. cierto falso		**7.** cierto falso		**12.** cierto falso	
3. cierto falso		**8.** cierto falso		**13.** cierto falso	
4. cierto falso		**9.** cierto falso		**14.** cierto falso	
5. cierto falso		**10.** cierto falso		**15.** cierto falso	

Realidades 1

Capítulo 2B

Nombre _____

Fecha _____

Hora _____

AUDIO

Actividad 6

Tomás suddenly realizes in the middle of his science class that the diskette with his entire class project on it is missing! He asks several people if they know where it is. Listen as different people tell Tomás where they think his diskette is. In the timeline, write what classroom he goes to and where in the classroom he looks, in the order in which you hear them. You will hear this conversation twice.

	Susana	Antonio	Noé	Sr. Atkins
Classroom				
Location in room				

Where did Tomás eventually find his diskette? _____

Actividad 7

It's time to take the Spanish Club picture for the yearbook, but there are several people who have still not arrived. Andrés, the president, decides to use his cell phone to find out where people are. As you listen to the first part of each conversation, complete the sentences below with the information he finds out. For example, you might write: **Beto está en el gimnasio.** You will hear each dialogue twice.

1. Los dos profesores de español _____.

2. Javier _____.

3. Alejandra y Sara _____.

4. Mateo _____.

5. José y Antonieta _____.

Nombre _____ Hora _____

Fecha _____

AUDIO

Actividad 8

One of your classmates from Spanish class is working in a store that sells school supplies. She overhears a customer speaking Spanish to his father, and decides to try out her Spanish. As she asks him what he wants to buy, she discovers that he never wants just one of anything. As the customer tells your classmate what he wants, write the items on the sales receipt below. Use the pictures below to calculate the price of his purchases. You will hear each conversation twice.

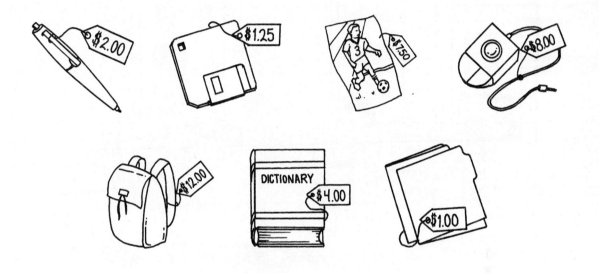

¿QUÉ NECESITA COMPRAR?	PRECIO
Modelo _Tres bolígrafos_	$6.00
1. _____	_____
2. _____	_____
3. _____	_____
4. _____	_____
5. _____	_____
6. _____	_____

Actividad 9

Listen to two friends talking outside the door of the Spanish Club meeting. They want to go to the meeting, but they are afraid they won't remember everyone's names. Look at the drawing. In the grid, write in the name of the person who is being described. You will hear each dialogue twice.

(A)	(B)	(C)
(D)	(E)	(F)

Realidades ❶

Capítulo 2B

Nombre _____

Fecha _____

Hora _____

WRITING

Actividad 10

After your first day of school, you are describing your classroom to your parents. Using the picture below, tell them how many of each object there are in the room. Follow the model.

Modelo *Hay un escritorio en la sala de clases.* _____

1. _____

2. _____

3. _____

4. _____

5. _____

6. _____

7. _____

Realidades ❶

Capítulo 2B

Nombre _____

Hora _____

Fecha _____

WRITING

Actividad 11

You are describing your classroom to your Spanish-speaking pen pal. Using complete sentences and the verb **estar**, tell what is in your room and where each item is located. Follow the model.

| Modelo | *Hay una mesa en la clase. Está al lado de la puerta.* |

1. _____

2. _____

3. _____

4. _____

5. _____

6. _____

7. _____

8. _____

Actividad 12

Answer the following questions about things you have for school. Use the pictures as a guide. Follow the model.

| Modelo | ¿Qué hay en la mochila? |

En la mochila hay unos lápices y bolígrafos. También hay una calculadora y dos libros: el libro de matemáticas y el libro de inglés.

Realidades **1**

Capítulo 2B

Nombre _____

Fecha _____

Hora _____

WRITING

1.   ¿Qué hay en la clase de ciencias sociales?

_____

_____

_____

_____

_____

2.   ¿Qué hay encima del escritorio? ¿Y al lado?
¿Y detrás?

_____

_____

_____

_____

_____

Realidades 1

Capítulo 2B

Nombre _____

Hora _____

Fecha _____

WRITING

Actividad 13

The two rooms pictured below were once identical, but Sala 2 has been rearranged. Look at each picture carefully. Circle seven items in Sala 2 that are different from Sala 1. Then, write sentences about how Sala 2 is different. Follow the model.

Sala 1 Sala 2

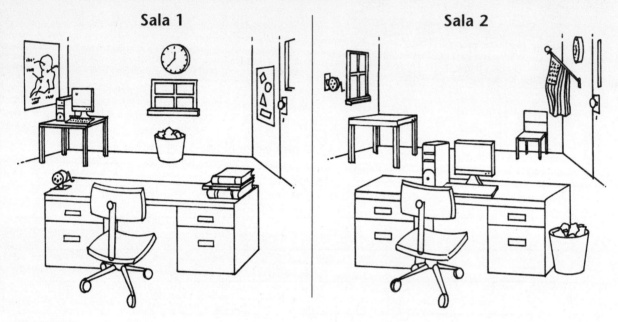

Modelo   *En la sala 2 no hay libros encima del escritorio.*

1. _____

_____

2. _____

_____

3. _____

_____

4. _____

_____

5. _____

_____

6. _____

_____

7. _____

_____

Antes de ver el video

Actividad 1

What do you like to eat for breakfast and lunch? Fill in the chart with that information.

Desayuno	Almuerzo

¿Comprendes?

Actividad 2

Think about the foods Rosa believes people in the United States eat for breakfast. What do Tomás and Raúl really eat?

1. ¿Qué come Tomás para el desayuno?

Tomás bebe _____ y come _____ para el desayuno.

2. Y, ¿qué come Raúl?

Raúl bebe _____ y _____ , come _____ , y a

veces también come un _____ .

Realidades ⓵

Capítulo 3A

Nombre _____

Hora _____

Fecha _____

VIDEO

Actividad 3

Although Rosa makes a big breakfast for Tomás that day, the family does not eat very much regularly. Answer the questions below.

1. ¿Quién prepara el desayuno? _____

2. Lorenzo: "Es mucha comida, ¿no? _____ ,

   _____ , _____ , _____ ,

   _____ ..." Rosa: "En los Estados Unidos, todos comen mucho en el

   desayuno."

3. Lorenzo: "Nosotros nunca comemos mucho en el desayuno,

   Rosa. Mira, yo sólo bebo un _____ y a veces como

   un _____ ."

4. Según Rosa, en los Estados Unidos comemos huevos, salchichas,

   tocino y pan tostado en el desayuno y _____

   _____ en el almuerzo.

Y, ¿qué más?

Actividad 4

Do you recall what you wrote in **Actividad** 1 about foods that you like to eat? Now that you have heard people in Costa Rica talk about what they eat, write down three questions of your own to ask a classmate about food. With a partner, ask your questions and compare answers.

¿_____?

¿_____?

¿_____?

Nombre _____

Hora _____

Fecha _____

Actividad 5

You are helping out a friend at the counter of Restaurante El Gaucho in Argentina. Listen to the orders and record the quantity of each item ordered by each customer in the appropriate box of the chart. You will hear each conversation twice.

RESTAURANTE EL GAUCHO

El almuerzo	Cliente 1	Cliente 2	Cliente 3	Cliente 4
Ensalada				
Hamburguesa				
Hamburguesa con queso				
Sándwich de jamón y queso				
Perro caliente				
Pizza				
Papas fritas				
Refresco				
Té helado				
Galletas				

Nombre _____ Hora _____

Fecha _____

Actividad 6

While working at the Hotel Buena Vista, you need to record breakfast orders for room service. Use the grid to make your report. First, listen carefully for the room number and write it in the appropriate box. Then write in the time requested. Finally, put a check mark next to each item ordered by the person in that room. You will hear each set of statements twice.

HOTEL BUENA VISTA

Número de habitación (*room number*)				
Hora de servicio				
Jugo de naranja				
Jugo de manzana				
Cereal				
Pan tostado				
Huevos				
Jamón				
Tocino				
Salchichas				
Yogur de fresas				
Café				
Café con leche				
Té				

Realidades ①

Capítulo 3A

Nombre _____

Hora _____

Fecha _____

AUDIO

Actividad 7

You are waiting in line at a restaurant counter. You hear people behind you talking about your friends. Listen carefully so you can figure out whom they're talking about. Pay close attention to verb and adjective endings. Put a check mark in the column after each conversation. You will hear each set of statements twice.

	Carlos	Gabriela	Carlos y sus amigos	Gabriela y sus amigas
1.	✓			✓
2.				✓
3.	✓			
4.			✓	
5.				✓
6.		✓		
7.			✓	

Actividad 8

Listen as actors from a popular Spanish soap opera are interviewed on the radio program called "**Las dietas de los famosos**" (*Diets of the Famous*). As you listen, write **sí** if the person mentions that he or she eats or drinks something most days. Write **no** if the person says that he or she never eats or drinks the item. You will hear this conversation twice.

	Lana Lote	Óscar Oso	Pepe Pluma	Tita Trompo

Nombre _____ Hora _____

Fecha _____

AUDIO

	Lana Lote	Óscar Oso	Pepe Pluma	Tita Trompo
🍓🍓🍓				
🍌				
🍔🍔				
🍟				
🌭🌭				
🍪🍪🍪				
🥗				
☕				
🍾				
☕				

Realidades ❶

Capítulo 3A

Nombre _____

Hora _____

Fecha _____

AUDIO

Actividad 9

Listen as the woman at the table next to you tries to help a child order from the menu. As you listen, check off the items on the menu that the child says he likes and those he dislikes. Then in the space provided, write what you think would be an "acceptable" lunch for him. You will hear this conversation twice.

	🍔	🍟	🥗	🌭	🥪	🍪	🥛	🥤
le gusta		✓				✓	✓	✓
no le gusta	✓		✓	✓	✓			

Un almuerzo bueno para Beto es _____

_____ .

Realidades 1

Capítulo 3A

Nombre _____

Fecha _____

Hora _____

WRITING

Actividad 10

You have decided to help your parents by doing the food shopping for the week. Your friend Rodrigo is helping you make the shopping list. Complete the conversation below using the picture and your own food preferences.

RODRIGO: ¿Qué hay de beber?

TÚ: _____

RODRIGO: ¿Quieres (*do you want*) algo más?

TÚ: _____

_____

RODRIGO: ¿Qué hay de comer para el desayuno?

TÚ: _____

RODRIGO: ¿Qué más quieres, entonces?

TÚ: _____

_____

RODRIGO: ¿Qué hay para el almuerzo?

TÚ: _____

RODRIGO: ¿Y quieres algo más?

TÚ: _____

_____

RODRIGO: ¿Y qué frutas necesitan?

TÚ :   _____

Realidades 1

Capítulo 3A

Nombre _____

Fecha _____

Hora _____

WRITING

Actividad 11

Describe each of the following scenes using as many **-er** and **-ir** verbs as you can. Use complete sentences.

_____

_____

_____

_____

yo   Ana y yo

tú   los estudiantes

_____

_____

_____

_____

Nombre _____

Hora _____

Fecha _____

WRITING

Actividad 12

In anticipation of your arrival in Spain next week, your host sister writes to ask you about your favorite foods. Complete your response below with sentences using the verbs **gustar** and **encantar**.

Estimada Margarita:

Gracias por su carta. Hay muchas comidas que me gustan. Para el desayuno,

_____. También

_____. Pero no

_____.

Pero me encanta más el almuerzo. Por ejemplo, _____

_____. También

_____. Pero no _____

_____.

¿Y a ti? ¿Te gustan las hamburguesas? ¿ _____

_____? ¿ _____

_____? ¿ _____

_____?

Nos vemos en una semana.

Un fuerte abrazo,

Melinda

Nombre _____   Hora _____

Fecha _____   **WRITING**

Actividad 13

The school nurse is teaching a class on nutrition and asks everyone to fill out a survey about what he or she eats. Using complete sentences, write your responses below.

1. ¿Qué comes y bebes en el desayuno?

_____

_____

_____

_____

_____

2. ¿Qué come y bebe tu familia en el almuerzo?

_____

_____

_____

_____

_____

3. ¿Qué comida te encanta?

_____

_____

_____

_____

_____

_____

Antes de ver el video

Actividad 1

Think about the typical diet of a teenager. Which foods are healthy choices and which ones are not? Make a list of five foods in each category.

Comida buena para la salud ☺

Comida mala para la salud ☹

_____   _____

_____   _____

_____   _____

_____   _____

_____   _____

¿Comprendes?

Actividad 2

Write the name of the person from the video who made each statement.

1. "El café de aquí es muy bueno." _____
2. "No, no; un refresco no; un jugo de fruta." _____
3. "En Costa Rica, un refresco es un jugo de fruta." _____
4. "Yo hago mucho ejercicio..." _____
5. "Aquí en San José, todos caminamos mucho." _____
6. "... aquí una soda no es una bebida; es un restaurante." _____
7. "Me encanta el gallo pinto." _____

Nombre _____ Hora _____

Fecha _____

VIDEO

Actividad 3

Answer the questions.

1. ¿Qué es muy importante para Costa Rica?

   _____

2. Según Raúl, ¿qué es bueno de Costa Rica?

   _____

3. Según Tomás, ¿qué es bueno para la salud?

   _____

4. ¿Qué hacen todos en San José?

   _____

5. ¿Qué más hacen en San José?

   _____

6. ¿Qué es una *soda* en Costa Rica?

   _____

Y, ¿qué más?

Actividad 4

Tomás was confused because he learned that **un refresco** was a soft drink. However, in Costa Rica **un refresco** is fruit juice. Can you think of any examples of English words that have a different meaning depending on where in the United States you go? What are their different meanings?

_____

_____

_____

_____

_____

_____

Actividad 5

Listen to a radio announcer as he interviews people at the mall about their lifestyles. Pay close attention to the things that they say they do and eat. What in their lifestyles is good or bad for their health? Match what they say to the pictures below. Then write the corresponding letter in the appropriate column. You will hear this conversation twice.

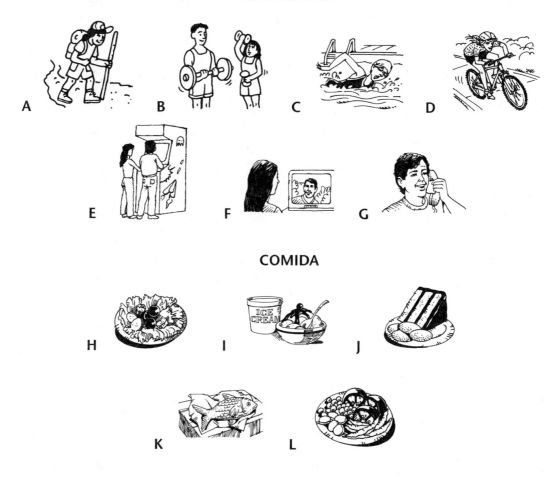

ACTIVIDADES

A   B   C   D

E   F   G

COMIDA

H   I   J

K   L

	Bueno para la salud ☺	Malo para la salud ☹
1. Mariana	_____	_____
2. Jorge	_____	_____
3. Luz	_____	_____
4. Nacho	_____	_____

Nombre _____ Hora _____

Fecha _____

AUDIO

Actividad 6

Listen as students in a health class in Costa Rica present a list of the "dos and don'ts" of staying healthy. Which are **consejos lógicos** (*logical advice*) and which are **consejos ridículos** (*ridiculous advice*)? Place a check mark in the appropriate box of the chart. You will hear each set of statements twice.

	1	2	3	4	5	6	7	8	9	10
Consejo lógico										
Consejo ridículo										

Actividad 7

A Spanish-speaking telemarketer calls your home to interview you about the food preferences of teens. He must have gotten your name from your Spanish teacher! He asks you to tell him whether you think certain food items are **malo** or **sabroso**. Be sure to listen carefully so that you will be able to use the correct form of the adjective for each item. Write what you would say in the spaces below. You will hear each question twice.

1. _____

2. _____

3. _____

4. _____

5. _____

6. _____

7. _____

8. _____

9. _____

10. _____

Realidades **1**

Capítulo 3B

Nombre _____

Fecha _____

Hora _____

AUDIO

Actividad 8

In an effort to improve food in the school cafeteria, students are asked to anonymously call in their opinions about school food. You are asked to chart the responses of the Spanish-speaking students. As you listen to their opinions, fill in the grid. If they say something positive about a particular menu item, put a plus sign in the appropriate column; if they say something negative, put a minus sign in the column. You will hear each set of statements twice.

1										
2										
3										
4										
5										

Actividad 9

Listen as people call in to ask Dr. Armando their health questions on his radio program **"Pregunte al doctor Armando."** While you listen to their questions and Dr. Armando's advice (**consejo**), fill in the chart below. Do you agree with his advice? You will hear this conversation twice.

NOMBRE	¿LA PREGUNTA?	EL CONSEJO
1. Beatriz		
2. Mauricio		
3. Loli		
4. Luis		

Nombre _____

Hora _____

Fecha _____

Actividad 10

A. The school nurse has compiled information on what everyone eats and is now telling you which foods are good for your health and which are not. Remember what you wrote for her survey? List the items you eat on a daily basis. Be sure to use words from the previous chapter as well as ones from this chapter.

_____ _____ _____
_____ _____ _____
_____ _____ _____
_____ _____ _____
_____ _____ _____

B. Now, use the nutrition pyramid shown and what you know about a well-balanced diet to fill in what the nurse would say. Follow the model.

Modelo *Los espaguetis son buenos para la salud. Ud. debe comer mucho pan y muchos cereales.*

1. _____
_____

2. _____
_____

3. _____
_____

4. _____
_____

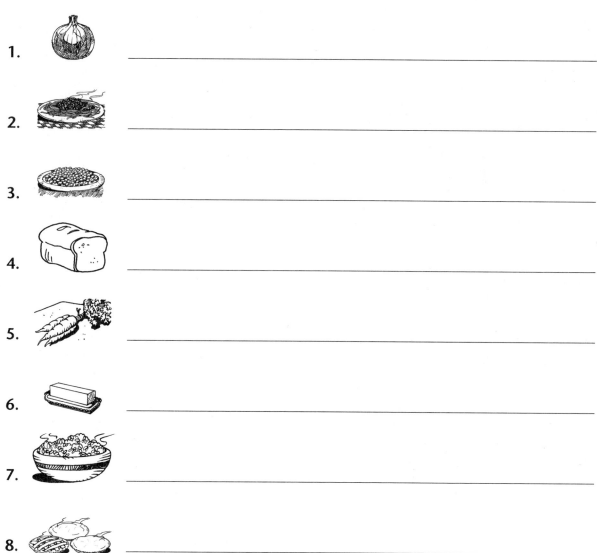

Realidades 1

Capítulo 3B

Nombre _____

Hora _____

Fecha _____

WRITING

Actividad 11

Write your opinions of the following foods. Use the correct forms of the following adjectives in your sentences.

bueno	malo	sabroso	divertido
malo para la salud		bueno para la salud	
	interesante		horrible

Modelo   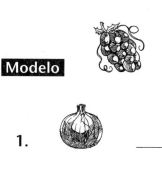   *Las uvas son sabrosas.* _____

1. _____

2. _____

3. _____

4. _____

5. _____

6. _____

7. _____

8. _____

Realidades 1

Capítulo 3B

Nombre _____

Hora _____

Fecha _____

WRITING

Actividad 12

Below you see three groups of friends sitting at tables in a cafeteria. Describe the people and items at each table.

Mesa 1:

_____

_____

_____

_____

Mesa 2:

_____

_____

_____

_____

Mesa 3:

_____

_____

_____

_____

Actividad 13

Write a letter to your Spanish-speaking pen pal about a restaurant that you and your parents like to go to for dinner. Tell what you and your family members normally eat and drink, what the food is like, and what the waiters (**camareros**) are like.

Estimado(a) _____ :

_____

_____

_____

_____

_____

_____

_____

_____

_____

_____

_____

_____

_____

_____

_____

_____

_____

_____

_____

Un abrazo,

_____

Nombre _____

Hora _____

Fecha _____

Antes de ver el video

Actividad 1

Think of activities you do at different times during the week. Make a list of four activities you do during the week and then four activities you do during the weekend.

Actividades durante la semana

_____

_____

_____

_____

Actividades durante el fin de semana

_____

_____

_____

_____

¿Comprendes?

Actividad 2

Javier has just moved to a new high school in Spain, and he is sitting by himself. Ignacio, Elena, and Ana try to find out more about him. What do they do, and what do they learn? Write **cierto** (*true*) or **falso** (*false*) next to each statement.

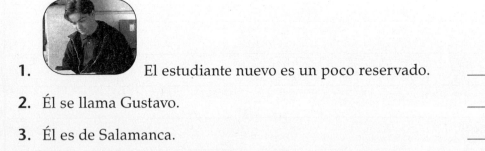

1. El estudiante nuevo es un poco reservado. _____

2. Él se llama Gustavo. _____

3. Él es de Salamanca. _____

4. Todos los días va a la biblioteca después de las clases. _____

5. Los tres amigos van a hablar con él. _____

6. A Javier le gusta practicar deportes. _____

Realidades 1

Capítulo 4A

Nombre _____

Fecha _____

Hora _____

VIDEO

7. A veces, él prefiere ir al cine a ver películas. _____

8. A él no le gusta hablar con su amigo Esteban de San Antonio. _____

Actividad 3

What do the new friends do after class? Fill the blanks with complete sentences.

Nuevos amigos	¿Adónde va después de las clases?
1. Javier	
2. Ignacio	
3. Elena	
4. Ana	

Y, ¿qué más?

Actividad 4

What do you do after school every day? What do you sometimes do, and what do you never do at all? Write a short paragraph about your afterschool activities, following the example below.

Modelo *Yo voy a mi trabajo todos los días en el centro comercial. A veces, voy con una amiga al cine después del trabajo. Nunca voy al gimnasio durante la semana.*

_____

_____

_____

Nombre _____   Hora _____

Fecha _____

AUDIO

Actividad 5

Listen as Lorena talks to Luis and Antonio about where they are going during the week. Under each picture in the grid, write in the name of Luis or Antonio if they tell Lorena they are going to that place. In some cases, you will fill in both of their names. After completing the grid, you will be able to complete the sentences under the grid. You will hear this conversation twice.

lunes							
martes							
miércoles							
jueves							
viernes							
sábado							
domingo							

1. Luis y Antonio van al (a la) _____ el _____.

2. También van al (a la) _____ el _____.

Realidades ❶

Capítulo 4A

Nombre _____

Fecha _____

Hora _____

AUDIO

Actividad 6

You are volunteering as a tour guide during the upcoming Hispanic Arts Festival in your community. To make sure you would be able to understand the following questions if a visitor were to ask them, write the number of the question under the correct picture that would correspond to a logical response. You can check your answers to see if you're ready to answer visitors' questions during the Festival. You will hear each question twice.

Actividad 7

Your friend Miguel calls his mother from your house to give her an update on his plans for the day. Just from listening to his side of the conversation, you realize that his mother has LOTS of questions. What does she ask him, based on Miguel's answers? Choose from the following:

A. ¿Adónde vas?   **D.** ¿Cómo es tu amigo?

B. ¿Con quiénes vas?   **E.** ¿Por qué van?

C. ¿Cuándo vas?

You will hear each set of statements twice.

1. _____   2. _____   3. _____   4. _____   5. _____

Realidades ①

Capítulo 4A

Nombre _____

Fecha _____

Hora _____

AUDIO

Actividad 8

The yearbook staff is identifying students' pictures for the yearbook. Look at the pictures from the class trip to Mexico. Listen to the conversations and write the names of Arturo, Susi, Gloria, Martín, David, Eugenia, Enrique, and Lucía under the correct pictures. You will hear each dialogue twice.

_____   _____   _____

_____   _____   _____

Actividad 9

Listen as a radio interviewer talks to Maricela, a young woman from Spain, about her city that was once home to the **Reyes** Fernando and Isabel. You will learn why it is such a popular tourist spot. After listening, answer the questions below. You will hear this conversation twice.

1. Maricela es de

    a) Madrid.   b) Aranjuez.   c) Barcelona.

2. La ciudad es famosa por

    a) el pescado.   b) el helado.   c) las fresas.

3. Los turistas van

    a) al palacio.   b) a las montañas.   c) a la playa.

4. La ciudad de Maricela está a unos _____ minutos de Madrid.

    a) quince   b) treinta   c) cincuenta

5. Las comidas típicas son

    a) pizza y espaguetis.   b) fresas y pasteles de manzana.   c) pollo y judías verdes.

6. Maricela va _____ para pasar tiempo con los amigos.

    a) al parque   b) al cine   c) a las montañas

Actividad 10

While on a hike one day, you stumble upon a "Wheel of the Future." When you spin this wheel, you will land on a picture of a place. The wheel will send you to that place if you tell it when you want to go and what you plan to do there. Write what you would tell the wheel for each place. Follow the model.

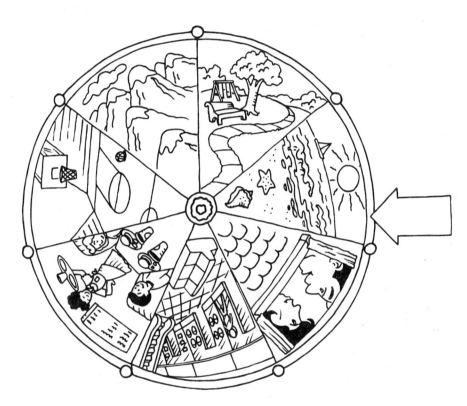

Modelo _Voy a la playa el viernes para nadar._

1. _____

2. _____

3. _____

4. _____

5. _____

6. _____

7. _____

Nombre _____

Hora _____

Fecha _____

WRITING

Actividad 11

You are having a surprise party for your best friend next weekend, and you need to know where your family and friends are going to be this week so that you can get in touch with them to make plans. Below is a planner containing information on everyone's plans for the week. Using the pictures to help you, write where your friends and family will be and what they will be doing on that day. Use the model as a guide.

Modelo

YO

Lunes: _El lunes yo voy a la biblioteca para hacer la tarea._

Tú

lunes _____

Geraldo

martes _____

Mi familia y Yo

miércoles _____

Juan y Tú

jueves _____

Pedro y Claudia

viernes _____

Mariana

sábado _____

Anita y Lucita

domingo _____

Nombre _____ Hora _____

Fecha _____

WRITING

Actividad 12

You are a contestant on a game show. The host of the show has given you these answers. Write the corresponding questions.

Modelo	El catorce de febrero

¿Cuándo es el Día de San Valentín? _____

1. El primer presidente de los Estados Unidos

_____

2. Al norte (*north*) de los Estados Unidos

_____

3. Usamos esta cosa para conectar al Internet.

_____

4. Muy bien, gracias. ¿Y tú?

_____

5. Vamos a la tienda para comprar frutas.

_____

6. Las personas que enseñan las clases

_____

7. Usamos estas partes del cuerpo para ver.

_____

Actividad 13

A. Write four complete sentences that tell about places you and a friend go to on the weekend.

1. _____

2. _____

3. _____

4. _____

Realidades ①

Capítulo 4A

Nombre _____

Hora _____

Fecha _____

WRITING

B. Now, use your sentences from Part A to write a paragraph telling with whom you go to these places, what the places are like, and what you do when you are there.

_____

_____

_____

_____

_____

_____

_____

_____

_____

_____

_____

_____

_____

_____

Realidades ①

Capítulo 4B

Nombre _____

Fecha _____

Hora _____

VIDEO

Antes de ver el video

Actividad 1

Think of activities you like to do. Here is a list of six activities. Rank them in order from your favorite to your least favorite, with 1 as your favorite and 6 as your least favorite.

_____ ir a bailar   _____ ir al cine a ver películas

_____ nadar   _____ montar en bicicleta

_____ estudiar en la biblioteca   _____ ir de compras al centro comercial

¿Comprendes?

Actividad 2

Ignacio, Javier, Elena, and Ana are playing soccer at the park. Who makes each statement? Write the name of the person who says each item on the line.

1. "Mañana juego al tenis con mis primos."   _____

2. "Yo también estoy muy cansada y tengo mucha sed."   _____

3. "Prefiero otros deportes, como el fútbol."   _____

4. "¿Sabes jugar también al vóleibol?"   _____

5. "También me gusta ir de pesca."   _____

6. "Puedes bailar conmigo…"   _____

7. "Lo siento. No sé bailar bien."   _____

8. "Voy a preparar un pastel fabuloso."   _____

VIDEO

Actividad 3

Look at the activities below, and circle the ones you saw or heard about while watching the video. Then, write the ones that Elena can do well on the lines below.

jugar al fútbol	jugar al tenis	ir de cámping	ir de pesca

ir a las fiestas   ver el partido   jugar al vóleibol

caminar en el parque   jugar al fútbol americano   practicar deportes

ir al concierto   preparar un pastel   jugar al béisbol   jugar al golf

jugar al básquetbol   bailar y cantar   tomar refrescos

_____

_____

Y, ¿qué mas?

Actividad 4

Imagine that Ignacio, Javier, Elena, and Ana want you to join them in their various activities. What answers might you give them? Respond to their invitations with some of the phrases from the video, or make up your own responses from what you have learned. Follow the model.

Modelo   ¿Quieres jugar al fútbol en el parque?

Sí, quiero jugar al fútbol en el parque, pero no juego muy bien.

1. ¿Puedes jugar al tenis mañana?

_____

2. Oye, juegas muy bien al vóleibol. ¿Puedes jugar más tarde?

_____

3. ¿Quieres ir con nosotros a la fiesta esta noche?

_____

4. ¿Sabes bailar?

_____

Realidades ①

Capítulo 4B

Nombre _____

Fecha _____

Hora _____

AUDIO

Actividad 5

There are not enough hours in the day to do everything we want to do. Listen to the following interviews. What do these people want more time to do? In the blanks provided, write the number of the statement that corresponds to each picture. You will hear each set of statements twice.

Actividad 6

After listening to each of the following statements, decide if you think the excuses given are believable (**creíble**) or unbelievable (**increíble**). Be prepared to defend your answers with a partner after making your decisions. You will hear each set of statements twice.

EXCUSAS, EXCUSAS

	Creíble	Increíble		Creíble	Increíble
1.	❑	❑	5.	❑	❑
2.	❑	❑	6.	❑	❑
3.	❑	❑	7.	❑	❑
4.	❑	❑	8.	❑	❑

Realidades ①

Capítulo 4B

Nombre _____

Fecha _____

Hora _____

AUDIO

Actividad 7

Listen to the following couple as they try to decide what they are going to do tonight. Every time an activity is mentioned that one of the two people is going to do, draw a circle around the picture. If the other person is NOT going to do that activity, draw an X through the picture. The pictures with circles only should represent what both people finally decide to do. You will hear each conversation twice.

Actividad 8

Listen as a radio program host interviews a fitness expert, doctora Benítez, about the best way to get in shape. Listen to the **entrevista** (*interview*), and choose the best answer to the questions below. You will hear this conversation twice.

1. ¿En qué es experta la doctora Benítez?

   a) deportes   b) cocinar   c) música   d) ejercicio y nutrición

2. Según la doctora, ¿cuántos minutos de ejercicio debes hacer todos los días?

   a) una hora   b) quince minutos   c) treinta minutos

3. Según Miguel, ¿por qué no puede hacer mucho ejercicio?

   a) Es demasiado perezoso.   b) Está muy ocupado.   c) Está triste.

4. ¿Qué es divertido para Miguel?

   a) jugar al tenis   b) ver la tele   c) jugar al fútbol

5. Después de jugar, ¿qué no debemos comer?

   a) cereales   b) frutas y verduras   c) pasteles

Nombre _____ Hora _____

Fecha _____ **AUDIO**

Actividad 9

Your Spanish teacher always encourages you to speak Spanish to your classmates outside of class. In order to do that, you and your friends agreed to talk on the phone and/or leave messages on each other's answering machines for at least a week. Listen to the messages your friends have left on your answering machine today. Based on the messages, decide a) where the person wants to go; b) what the person wants to do; c) what time the person wants to go. Use the chart below to record the information. You will hear each set of statements twice.

	¿Adónde quiere ir?	¿Qué quiere hacer?	¿A qué hora quiere ir?
Justo			
Eva			
José			
Margarita			
Pedro			

Realidades ①

Capítulo 4B

Nombre _____

Fecha _____

Hora _____

WRITING

Actividad 10

A. Read the following announcements of upcoming events in Madrid. Underneath each announcement, write whether or not you are going to each event and why or why not.

UNA NOCHE DE ÓPERA ITALIANA

PRESENTANDO a **JOSÉ CARRERAS** en el Auditorio Nacional de Música, Madrid

el viernes a las siete de la noche

PARTIDO DE FÚTBOL

REAL BETIS CONTRA REAL MADRID

el domingo a las dos de la tarde en el Estadio Santiago Bernabeu

---

_____

_____

_____

_____

Fiesta Deportiva

¿Te gusta practicar deportes? ¿Eres atlético?

Ven a mi fiesta deportiva y puedes jugar varios deportes con muchas personas.

La fiesta es desde el viernes a las cinco de la tarde hasta el lunes a las cinco de la mañana.

_____

B. Now, in the spaces below, write whether five people you know are going to any one of the events and why or why not. Follow the model.

Modelo   *Mi amiga Ana va al partido de fútbol porque le gusta mucho el fútbol.*

   Mi amigo Ronaldo no va al concierto porque no le gusta la ópera.

1. _____

2. _____

3. _____

4. _____

5. _____

Nombre _____ Hora _____

Fecha _____

Actividad 11

Every time a classmate asks Eugenio if he wants to do something fun, he declines and gives a different excuse. In the spaces below, write the question that each classmate asks and Eugenio's varying answers. Follow the model.

Modelo

—*¿Vas a levantar pesas conmigo?* _____

—*No, no puedo levantar pesas porque me duele la cabeza.*

1. —¿ _____ ?

   —No, _____ .

2. —¿ _____ ?

   —No, _____ .

3. —¿ _____ ?

   —No, _____ .

4. —¿ _____ ?

   —No, _____ .

5. —¿ _____ ?

   —No, _____ .

6. —¿ _____ ?

   —No, _____ .

7. —¿ _____ ?

   —No, _____ .

Realidades ❶

Capítulo 4B

Nombre _____

Fecha _____

Hora _____

WRITING

Actividad 12

When put in the right order, each set of blocks below will ask a question. Unscramble the blocks by writing the contents of each block in the blank boxes. Then, answer the questions in the space provided.

1.

| J U E G | D E | E P O R | O S | F | U É | D | A S | L |
| INES | ¿ A Q | T E S | N A ? | S E M A | | | | |

_____

_____

2.

| ¿ A Q | M I G O | T E S | U S | A | J U E G | U É | D |
| S ? | A N | T E P O R | | | | | |

_____

_____

3.

| G A ? | L | E S | F A V O | ¿ C U Á | R I T O | J U E |
| R T E | U I É N | Y Q | T U | D E P O | | |

_____

_____

Realidades 1

Capítulo 4B

Nombre _____

Fecha _____

Hora _____

WRITING

Actividad 13

You are having a mid-semester party.

A. First, fill in the invitation below with the information about your party.

FIESTA DE MEDIO SEMESTRE

Lugar: _____

Hora: _____

Comida: _____

_____

RSVP: _____

B. Since you don't have everyone's mailing address, you have to e-mail some people about the party. Write your e-mail below. In addition to inviting them, tell them what activities you will have at the party, and where your house is (**está cerca de la biblioteca,** etc.).

Estimados amigos:

_____

_____

_____

_____

_____

_____

_____

_____

¡Me gustaría ver a todos en la fiesta!

Un fuerte abrazo,

_____

Nombre _____

Hora _____

Fecha _____

VIDEO

Antes de ver el video

Actividad 1

Look at this family tree. Label each person with his or her relationship to Ricardo.

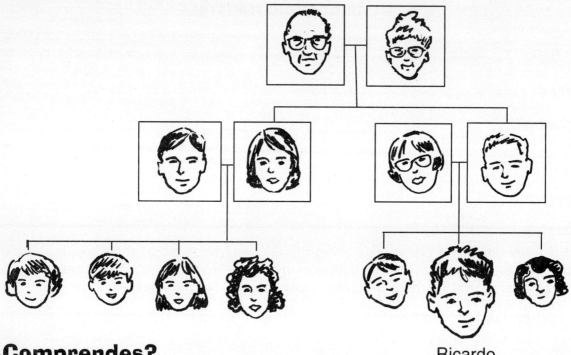

Ricardo

¿Comprendes?

Actividad 2

Cristina had a birthday party with some of her family members. How much do you remember about that party? Write **cierto** or **falso** next to each statement.

1. Angélica hace un video de la fiesta de su hermano. _____

2. El papá de Cristina saca fotos de la fiesta. _____

3. A Gabriel le gustan los deportes. _____

4. El perro de Cristina se llama Piñata. _____

5. La abuela de Cristina decora la fiesta con papel picado. _____

6. Capitán es muy sociable, le encanta estar con la familia. _____

7. Carolina es la hermana de Gabriel y Angélica. _____

8. Ricardo es el abuelo de Esteban. _____

Actividad 3

Who is being described? Write his or her name next to the description.

	Description	Name

1. esposa de Ricardo _____

2. tío de Cristina _____

3. hermana de Gabriel _____

4. esposa de Andrés _____

5. primo de Angélica _____

6. hermana mayor de Esteban _____

7. abuelo de Cristina _____

Nombre _____   Hora _____

Fecha _____

VIDEO

Y, ¿qué más?

Actividad 4

At Cristina's party we met many family members. Why don't you introduce your family, too? Write three sentences about your family or a family you know well. Follow the examples below.

Yo vivo en mi casa con mi mamá y mi hermano.

TÚ: _____

Mi hermano se llama Martín y tiene 10 años.

TÚ: _____

Yo tengo muchos primos y primas.

TÚ: _____

The lyrics for "Las mañanitas" as sung on the video are:

Éstas son las mañanitas que cantaba el rey David
a las muchachas bonitas, te las cantamos a ti.
Despierta, mi bien, despierta, mira que ya amaneció,
ya los pajarillos cantan, la luna ya se metió.

These are the early morning birthday songs
that King David used to sing
to pretty girls, and so we sing them to you.
Wake up, my dear, wake up, look, dawn has already come,
the little birds are singing, the moon is gone.

Realidades ❶

Capítulo 5A

Nombre _____

Hora _____

Fecha _____

AUDIO

Actividad 5

Beto is showing Raúl a picture of his family at a birthday party. Identify as many people as you can and write their names and relationship to Beto under the pictures. If Beto refers to a pet, simply write the pet's name under the picture. You will hear this conversation twice.

_____ _____ _____

_____ _____ _____

_____ _____ _____

_____ _____ _____

_____ _____ _____

_____ _____ _____

Actividad 6

You are chosen to participate in a popular radio quiz show on a local Spanish radio station. When it is your turn, you are happy to hear that your questions are in the category of **FAMILIA**. See if you can answer all of the questions correctly on the entry card below. Each question becomes a little more difficult. You will hear each set of questions twice.

1. _____

2. _____

3. _____

4. _____

5. _____

Actividad 7

Listen as three brothers talk to their mother after school. Try to fill in all of the squares in the grid with the correct information about Julio, Mateo, and Víctor. Remember, you might not hear the information given in the same order as it appears in the grid. You will hear this conversation twice.

	¿Cuántos años tiene?	¿Qué le gusta hacer?	¿Qué tiene que hacer?	¿Qué tiene en la mochila?
Julio				
Mateo				
Víctor				

Realidades **1**

Capítulo 5A

Nombre _____

Hora _____

Fecha _____

AUDIO

Actividad 8

Listen as two students tell their host families in Chile about their own families back home. As you listen to both of them, see if you can tell which family is being described. Put a check mark in the appropriate box on the grid. You will hear each set of statements twice.

La familia Gómez

La familia Sora

	1	2	3	4	5	6	7	8
La familia Gómez								
La familia Sora								

Nombre _____

Hora _____

Fecha _____

AUDIO

Actividad 9

Listen to the following phone calls to Ana, a favorite local talk show host. Each caller has a problem with someone in his or her family. As you listen to each caller, take notes on his or her problems. After all of the callers have spoken, write a sentence of advice for each caller. You may write your advice in English. You will hear set of statements twice.

	PROBLEMA	CONSEJO
Maritza		
Armando		
Andrés		
María Luisa		

Nombre _____   Hora _____

Fecha _____   **WRITING**

Actividad 10

Look at the pages from the Rulfo family photo album below. Then, write one or two sentences describing the people in each photo. What is their relationship to each other? What do you think they are like, based on the pictures?

Juanito, Lolita y Pepe

Pepe, Marcos, Romana, Timoteo y Luisita

"El cumpleaños de Rafael"

1. Foto 1

_____

_____

2. Foto 2

_____

_____

3. Foto 3

_____

_____

Realidades 1

Capítulo 5A

Nombre _____

Fecha _____

Hora _____

WRITING

Actividad 11

People have many obligations during the day. Using **tener que**, write what you think the following people have to do at the time of day or place given. Follow the model.

Modelo   mi padre / a las 7:00 de la mañana

Mi padre tiene que desayunar a las siete de la mañana.

1. yo / a las 7:30 de la mañana

_____

2. tú / en la clase de español

_____

3. los estudiantes / en la clase de inglés

_____

4. el profesor / en la clase de matemáticas

_____

5. las personas de la escuela / a las doce de la tarde (al mediodía)

_____

6. Uds. / en la clase de arte

_____

7. los estudiantes malos / en la clase de educación física

_____

8. mi amigo / a las 3:00 de la tarde

_____

9. mis hermanos y yo / a las 5:00 de la tarde

_____

10. mi familia / a las 6:00 de la tarde

_____

Realidades ①

Capítulo 5A

Nombre _____

Hora _____

Fecha _____

WRITING

Actividad 12

A. Your family tree is very complex. It takes many links to connect everyone in the family. Using possessive adjectives, write 10 sentences about how people are related in your family. Use the model to help you.

Modelo _Mi tío tiene dos hijos._ _____

Mi abuelo es el padre de mi tía. _____

1. _____
2. _____
3. _____
4. _____
5. _____
6. _____
7. _____
8. _____
9. _____
10. _____

B. Now, draw your family tree.

Realidades 1

Capítulo 5A

Nombre _____

Fecha _____

Hora _____

WRITING

Actividad 13

Your pen pal from Argentina has asked you to tell her about a member of your family. First, tell her the person's name, age, and relationship to you. Then, describe what the person is like.

Once you finish writing, read your description and check to make sure that all the words are spelled correctly and that you have used accents where necessary. Also, check to make sure the endings of the adjectives agree with the nouns they are describing.

Hola, Ana Sofía:

_____

_____

_____

_____

_____

_____

_____

_____

_____

_____

_____

Saludos,

_____

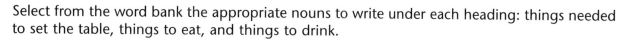

VIDEO

Antes de ver el video

Actividad 1

Select from the word bank the appropriate nouns to write under each heading: things needed to set the table, things to eat, and things to drink.

menú	tacos	tenedor	flan
enchiladas	limonada	servilleta	postre
café	refresco	cuchillo	jugo de naranja

Para poner la mesa

_____

_____

_____

_____

Para comer

_____

_____

_____

_____

Para beber

_____

_____

_____

_____

¿Comprendes?

Actividad 2

Angélica's family is having dinner at the restaurant **México Lindo**. Find the best choice to complete each statement by writing the letter in the space provided.

1. El camarero está nervioso; _____
   a. tiene mucho trabajo.
   b. es su primer día de trabajo.
   c. tiene sueño.

2. El papá de Angélica pide un té helado _____
   a. porque tiene calor.
   b. porque es delicioso.
   c. porque tiene frío.

3. La mamá de Angélica pide de postre _____

     a. arroz con pollo.

     b. tacos de bistec.

     c. flan.

4. La mamá de Angélica necesita _____

     a. una servilleta.

     b. el menú.

     c. un cuchillo y un tenedor.

Actividad 3

Match each person with the things he or she ordered. Write the letter of the foods and beverages in the spaces provided.

1. Mamá _____   a. jugo de naranja y fajitas de pollo

2. Angélica _____   b. enchiladas

3. Papá _____   c. café, ensalada de frutas y flan

4. Esteban _____   d. té helado, tacos de bistec y café

5. Cristina _____   e. refresco y arroz con pollo

6. Sr. del pelo castaño _____   f. hamburguesa y refresco

Y, ¿qué más?

Actividad 4

You and your friend Graciela are having dinner at a Mexican restaurant with your family. Graciela doesn't speak Spanish, so your mom orders dinner for her. Then, you give your order. Look at the menu to see your options, then write your order in the space provided in the dialogue below.

	MENÚ	
BEBIDAS	**PLATO PRINCIPAL**	**POSTRES**
Refrescos	Enchiladas	Flan
Jugo de naranja	Tacos de carne/pollo	Helado
Té helado/caliente	Fajitas de carne/pollo	Frutas frescas
Café	Burritos	

CAMARERO: ¿Qué van a pedir para beber?

MAMÁ: La joven quiere un jugo de naranja, y yo quiero un refresco.

TÚ: _____

CAMARERO: ¿Qué quieren pedir para el plato principal?

MAMÁ: Para la joven enchiladas, y yo quiero arroz con pollo.

TÚ: _____

CAMARERO: ¿Quieren pedir algo de postre?

MAMÁ: Para la joven un flan. Yo no quiero nada, gracias.

TÚ: _____

Actividad 5

You are delighted to find out that you can understand a conversation that a family at a table near you in a restaurant is having in Spanish. The family doesn't seem very happy with the waiter. Listen to find out what each family member is upset about. By looking at the pictures in the grid below, check off the item that is causing the problem. You will hear each conversation twice.

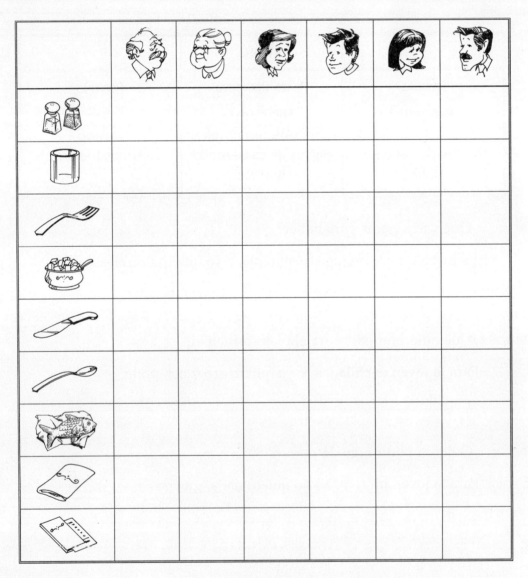

Actividad 6

Five young people go to a department store to buy hats (**sombreros**) as presents for their friends. Listen as each person describes the person he or she is buying the present for. Write the name of each person described under the hat that best matches that person. You will hear each conversation twice.

Realidades 1

Capítulo 5B

Nombre _____

Hora _____

Fecha _____

AUDIO

sociable, deportista, atrevido(a)

_____

romántico(a), talentoso(a), paciente

_____

serio(a), trabajador(a), práctico(a)

_____

elegante, divertido(a), simpático(a)

_____

aventurero(a), atrevido(a), interesante

_____

Actividad 7

Listen as a group of friends discuss Julia's upcoming surprise birthday party. Look at the list of party items. Write the name of each person next to the item that he or she is bringing. Circle any item that still needs to be assigned. You will hear this conversation twice.

Los platos _____ Los refrescos _____ Las servilletas _____

Los vasos _____ Los globos _____ El postre _____

Los tenedores _____ La piñata _____ Las flores _____

Las cucharas _____ Las luces _____ El helado _____

Actividad 8

Iván knows many different people from various places. Listen to him describe these people. Fill in the chart as you hear each piece of information given. You will hear each set of statements twice.

	¿De dónde es/son?	¿Dónde está(n)?	¿Está(n) contento/a/os/as?
Juanita			
Los tíos			
Iván y su familia			
Felipe			
Juanita y Julie			

Realidades ①   Nombre _____   Hora _____

Capítulo 5B   Fecha _____   **AUDIO**

Actividad 9

Listen as a girl describes a photo of a party to her friend who was unable to attend. Write the names of each person described on the line that corresponds to each picture. You will hear the dialogues twice.

A. _____   D. _____

B. _____   E. _____

C. _____   F. _____

Realidades 1

Capítulo 5B

Nombre _____

Hora _____

Fecha _____

WRITING

Actividad 10

Draw a picture of yourself and three other people in your family. Then, write a description of the person below each picture. You can draw imaginary family members if you prefer.

1.

_____ Yo _____

_____
_____
_____
_____
_____
_____
_____
_____

2.

_____

_____
_____
_____
_____
_____
_____
_____
_____

3.

_____

_____
_____
_____
_____
_____
_____
_____
_____

4.

_____

_____
_____
_____
_____
_____
_____
_____
_____

Realidades 1

Capítulo 5B

Nombre _____

Fecha _____

Hora _____

WRITING

Actividad 11

In preparation for their upcoming party, Juan and Elisa are talking on the phone about who is coming and what each guest is bringing. Read Elisa's guest list below, then complete the friends' conversation by writing sentences that include the correct form of either **venir** or **traer**.

Nuestra fiesta

Anita - la pizza
Pablo y José - la salsa
Jorge y Marta - la limonada y los refrescos
Luisa y Marcos - las galletas de chocolate
Nosotros - la carne

JUAN: ¿Anita viene a la fiesta el sábado?

ELISA: _____.

JUAN: ¡Qué bien! ¿También van a venir Pablo y José?

ELISA: Sí. Ellos _____.

JUAN: ¿Qué traen ellos?

ELISA: _____.

JUAN: Bien. Y ¿quién trae las bebidas?

ELISA: Pues, _____.

JUAN: Sí. Ahora, ¿quiénes traen el postre?

ELISA: _____.

JUAN: ¡Perfecto! ¿Y nosotros? ¿_____?

ELISA: ¡Traemos la carne, por supuesto!

Realidades 1

Capítulo 5B

Nombre _____

Hora _____

Fecha _____

WRITING

Actividad 12

Describe the following people. Consider their mood and location, their personality and appearance. Be creative and use the pictures and model to help you.

Modelo

Él es joven. Su pelo es corto y negro.

Es un chico estudioso.

Está en casa ahora porque está enfermo.

1. _____
   _____
   _____
   _____

2. _____
   _____
   _____
   _____

3. _____
   _____
   _____
   _____

4. _____
   _____
   _____
   _____

WRITING

Actividad 13

There is going to be a picnic at your new house, and your mother is telling you who is coming and what he or she will be bringing. Write what your mother says, using a name, a description word, and an item from the columns below. Use either **venir** or **traer** in your sentence. Use the names only once. Follow the model.

Nombre	Descripción	Va a traer
Los Sres. Vázquez	viejo	platos
	joven	tenedores
La Srta. Espinosa	contento	vasos
	simpático	pollo
Antonio Jerez	artístico	hamburguesas
	pelirrojo	pasteles
Fernando y María Sosa	enfermo	servilletas
	guapo	limonada
Catalina de la Cuesta	alto	cuchillos
	bajo	tazas

Modelo   *La señorita Espinosa viene a la fiesta. Ella es la mujer joven y simpática que vive cerca de nuestra casa. Ella siempre está contenta y trae los pasteles.*

1. _____

_____

2. _____

_____

3. _____

_____

4. _____

_____

Realidades ①

Capítulo 6A

Nombre _____

Fecha _____

Hora _____

VIDEO

Antes de ver el video

Actividad 1

Make a list of five items in your bedroom and five adjectives that describe your bedroom.

Cosas en mi dormitorio

_____

_____

_____

_____

_____

Descripción de mi dormitorio

_____

_____

_____

_____

_____

¿Comprendes?

Actividad 2

Below are some words and phrases that you have learned so far. On the lines below, write only the words that you most likely heard in the video episode about Ignacio's room.

a veces	ratón	bistec	¿A qué hora?	almuerzo
foto	desordenado	lámpara	pequeños	estante
pared	bueno	casa	mochila	peor
abuelos	bailar	cuarto	bicicleta	escritorio
calculadora	¿Adónde?	fiesta	discos compactos	color

_____ _____ _____

_____ _____ _____

_____ _____ _____

_____ _____ _____

_____ _____ _____

VIDEO

Actividad 3

Put the following scenes from the video in chronological order by numbering them from 1–7.

_____

_____

_____

_____

_____

_____

_____

Realidades 1

Capítulo 6A

Nombre _____

Hora _____

Fecha _____

VIDEO

Y, ¿qué más?

Actividad 4

What is your room like? Is it messy or neat? What do you have to the left and to the right of the room? What do you have on the wall, on the nightstand, or on a bookshelf? Can you compare your room to someone else's? Describe your room, using as much new vocabulary as you can. Follow the sample paragraph below.

Modelo

Mi cuarto es menos ordenado que el cuarto de mi hermana. A la izquierda tengo un estante, muy desordenado, con discos compactos. A la derecha está mi escritorio con libros y revistas. Tengo una foto de mi familia en la pared. También tengo otra foto de mi hermana en su cuarto, ¡y está ordenado!

_____

_____

_____

_____

_____

_____

_____

Nombre _____

Hora _____

Fecha _____

AUDIO

Actividad 5

Marta and her sister Ana have very similar bedrooms. However, since they have unique personalities and tastes, there are some differences! For each statement you hear, check off in the appropriate column whose bedroom is being described. You will hear each statement twice.

El dormitorio de Marta

El dormitorio de Ana

	Marta	Ana			Marta	Ana
1.	❑	❑	6.		❑	❑
2.	❑	❑	7.		❑	❑
3.	❑	❑	8.		❑	❑
4.	❑	❑	9.		❑	❑
5.	❑	❑	10.		❑	❑

Nombre _____ Hora _____

Fecha _____

AUDIO

Actividad 6

Your Spanish teacher asks you to represent your school at a local university's **Competencia Escolar** (*Scholastic Competition*) for secondary Spanish students. She gives you a tape to practice with for the competition. As you listen to the recording, decide whether the statement is true or false and mark it in the grid. You will hear each set of statements twice.

	1	2	3	4	5	6	7	8	9	10
Cierto										
Falso										

Actividad 7

Sra. Harding's class is planning an Immersion Weekend for the school district's Spanish students. Listen as four committee members discuss the best food to have, the best activities for younger and older students, and the best colors for the t-shirt (**camiseta**) that will be given to all participants. To keep track of what everyone thinks, fill in the grid. You will hear each set of statements twice.

	La mejor comida	Las actividades para los estudiantes menores	Las actividades para los estudiantes mayores	El mejor color para la camiseta
1				
2				
3				
4				

Actividad 8

Your friend is babysitting for a family with an eight-year-old boy and a ten-year-old girl. Since they are a Spanish-speaking family, your friend wants you to go with her in case she doesn't understand everything that the mother tells her. Listen to the conversation to learn all the ground rules. Write either **sí** or **no** in each column that matches what the mother says that the boy or girl can do. Be sure to write **no** in both columns if neither is allowed to do it. Write **sí** in both columns if both are allowed to do it. You will hear this conversation twice.

Realidades ❶

Capítulo 6A

Nombre _____

Fecha _____

Hora _____

AUDIO

Actividad 9

Look at the pictures in the chart below as you hear people describe their friends' bedrooms. Place a check in the chart that corresponds to all of the items mentioned by the friend. You will hear each set of statements twice.

	Javier	Sara	María	Marcos

WRITING

Actividad 10

Answer the following questions about your bedroom in complete sentences. If you prefer, you may write about your ideal bedroom.

1. ¿Cuál es tu color favorito?

   _____

2. ¿De qué color es tu dormitorio?

   _____

3. ¿Tienes una alfombra en tu dormitorio? ¿De qué color es?

   _____

4. ¿Tienes un despertador? ¿Cuándo usas tu despertador?

   _____

   _____

5. ¿Qué muebles (*furniture*) tienes en tu dormitorio?

   _____

   _____

6. ¿Qué cosas electrónicas tienes en tu dormitorio?

   _____

7. ¿Prefieres los videos o los DVDs? ¿Cuántos tienes?

   _____

8. ¿Cuántos discos compactos tienes?

   _____

WRITING

Actividad 11

A. Draw your bedroom or your ideal bedroom (including furniture, electronics, windows, books, decorations, and other possessions) in the space provided below.

 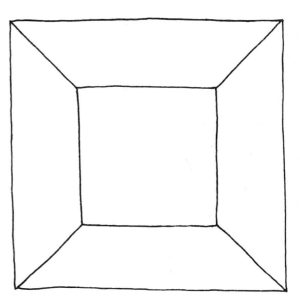

B. Now, compare the room that you drew with Juan's room on the left. Use the correct form of some of the following adjectives, or think of others: **práctico**, **interesante**, **grande**, **pequeño**, **mejor**, **peor**, **bonito**, **ordenado**.

Modelo	*Mi dormitorio es menos interesante que el dormitorio de Juan.*

1. _____

2. _____

3. _____

4. _____

5. _____

6. _____

Nombre _____ Hora _____

Fecha _____

WRITING

Actividad 12

You and your friends are comparing your English classes to determine which teacher's class to take next year. Read the information below, then compare the classes based on the criteria indicated. Follow the model.

	Clase A	**Clase B**	**Clase C**
Hora	Primera	Tercera	Octava
Profesor(a)	Profesora Brown — interesante	Profesor Martí — aburrido	Profesor Nicólas — muy interesante
Número de estudiantes	25	20	22
Dificultad	Difícil	Muy difícil	Fácil
Libros	Muy buenos	Aburridos	Buenos
Opinión general	A	B –	A–

Modelo Profesor *El profesor Martí es el menos interesante de los tres profesores.*

1. Hora (*temprano* or *tarde*)

   _____

2. Número de estudiantes (*grande* or *pequeña)*

   _____

3. Dificultad (*fácil* or *difícil*)

   _____

4. Libros (*buenos* or *malos*)

   _____

5. Opinión general (*mejor* or *peor*)

   _____

Realidades 1

Capítulo 6A

Nombre _____

Hora _____

Fecha _____

WRITING

Actividad 13

Your parents are hosting a family reunion, and nine extra people will be sleeping at your house. On the lines below, write where nine guests would sleep at your house. You may use your imagination if you prefer.

1. _____
   _____

2. _____
   _____

3. _____
   _____

4. _____
   _____

5. _____
   _____

6. _____
   _____

7. _____
   _____

8. _____
   _____

9. _____
   _____

Realidades 1

Capítulo 6B

Nombre _____

Hora _____

Fecha _____

VIDEO

Antes de ver el video

Actividad 1

Think of five chores you do at home. Then, write whether you like or don't like doing them using **me gusta** and **no me gusta nada**. Follow the model.

Modelo   *No me gusta nada limpiar mi dormitorio.* _____

1. _____

2. _____

3. _____

4. _____

5. _____

¿Comprendes?

Actividad 2

As you know from the video, Jorgito does all of the chores even though some were Elena's responsibility. Next to each chore listed below, tell whether it was Elena's responsibility or Jorgito's responsibility by writing the appropriate name in the space provided.

1. _____   quitar el polvo

2. _____   poner la mesa del comedor

3. _____   lavar los platos en la cocina

4. _____   hacer la cama en el dormitorio de Jorge

5. _____   hacer la cama en el cuarto de Elena

6. _____   arreglar el dormitorio de Jorge

7. _____   pasar la aspiradora

8. _____   dar de comer al perro

Nombre _____

Hora _____

Fecha _____

VIDEO

Actividad 3

Use the stills below from the video to help you answer the questions. Use complete sentences.

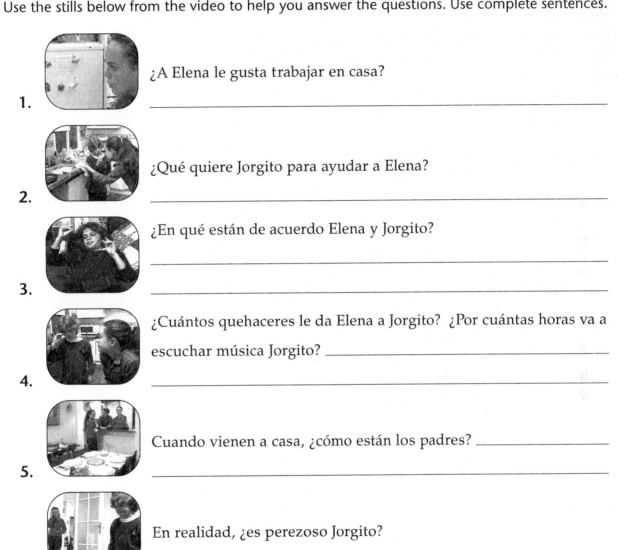

1. ¿A Elena le gusta trabajar en casa?

   _____

2. ¿Qué quiere Jorgito para ayudar a Elena?

   _____

3. ¿En qué están de acuerdo Elena y Jorgito?

   _____

   _____

4. ¿Cuántos quehaceres le da Elena a Jorgito? ¿Por cuántas horas va a

   escuchar música Jorgito? _____

   _____

5. Cuando vienen a casa, ¿cómo están los padres? _____

   _____

6. En realidad, ¿es perezoso Jorgito?

   _____

Realidades 1

Capítulo 6B

Nombre _____

Fecha _____

Hora _____

VIDEO

Y, ¿qué más?

Actividad 4

What activities might you do in each of these rooms? From the list in the box below, name at least two things that you might logically do in each room. Each activity should be used only once.

hacer la cama   pasar la aspiradora   escuchar música   cocinar la comida   poner la mesa   lavar los platos   quitar el polvo   comer la cena   arreglar el dormitorio desordenado   hacer la tarea

1. dormitorio de Elena

_____   _____

2. sala

_____   _____

3. comedor

_____   _____

4. cocina

_____   _____

5. dormitorio de Jorge

_____   _____

Realidades ❶

Capítulo 6B

Nombre _____

Hora _____

Fecha _____

AUDIO

Actividad 5

Listen as people look for things they have misplaced somewhere in their house. After each conversation, complete the sentence that explains what each person is looking for (**busca**) and in which room it is found. You will hear each dialogue twice.

1. La muchacha busca _____.

   Está en _____.

2. El muchacho busca _____.

   Está en _____.

3. La mujer busca _____.

   Está en _____.

4. El muchacho busca _____.

   Está en _____.

5. La muchacha busca _____.

   Está en _____.

Actividad 6

Señor Morales's nephew, Paco, volunteers to help his uncle move into a new apartment. However, Señor Morales is very distracted as he tells Paco where to put different things. Listen as he gives his nephew instructions and record in the grid below whether you think what he tells him to do each time is **lógico** (logical) **o ilógico** (illogical). You will hear each dialogue twice.

	1	2	3	4	5	6	7	8	9	10
lógico										
ilógico										

Actividad 7

Nico's parents are shocked when they come home from a trip to find that he hasn't done any of the chores that he promised to do. As they tell Nico what he needs to do, fill in the blanks below each picture with the corresponding number. You will hear each set of statements twice.

Actividad 8

Listen as each person rings a friend's doorbell and is told by the person who answers the door what the friend is doing at the moment. Based on that information, in which room of the house would you find the friend? As you listen to the conversations, look at the drawing of the house and write the number of the room that you think each friend might be in. You will hear each dialogue twice.

1. _____
2. _____
3. _____
4. _____
5. _____
6. _____

Realidades 1

Capítulo 6B

Nombre _____

Fecha _____

Hora _____

AUDIO

Actividad 9

Some people always seem to get out of doing their chores at home. Listen as a few teens tell their parents why they should not or cannot do what their parents have asked them to do. As you listen, write in the chart below what the parent requests, such as **lavar los platos**. Then write in the teens' excuses, such as **está lavando el coche**. You will hear each conversation twice.

	Los quehaceres	Las excusas
Marcos		
Luis		
Marisol		
Jorge		
Elisa		

Nombre _____ Hora _____

Fecha _____

WRITING

Actividad 10

The Justino family is getting ready for their houseguests to arrive. Help Sra. Justino write the family's to-do list. Follow the model.

Modelo

En el dormitorio, tenemos que quitar el polvo,
arreglar el cuarto y pasar la aspiradora.

1. _____

2. _____

3. _____

4. _____

Actividad 11

The Boteros's son is going to stay with his grandmother in Puerto Rico for a month. His parents want to make sure that he is well-behaved and helps out around the house. Write ten commands the Boteros might give to their son. Follow the model.

Modelo *Ayuda en la cocina, hijo.* _____

1. _____

2. _____

3. _____

4. _____

5. _____

6. _____

7. _____

8. _____

9. _____

10. _____

Nombre _____

Hora _____

Fecha _____

WRITING

Actividad 12

The Galgo family is very busy on Sunday. Look at their schedule below and write what each family member is doing at the time given. Use your imagination, and use the model to help you.

	10:00	12:00	3:00	8:00
La Señora Galgo	hacer ejercicio	almorzar	trabajar	dormir
El Señor Galgo	trabajar	cortar el césped	preparar la cena	jugar al tenis
Rodrigo	arreglar el cuarto	comer	tocar la guitarra	estudiar
Mariana	nadar	poner la mesa	leer	ver la tele

Modelo   12:00   *A las doce, la Sra. Galgo está almorzando con sus amigos y el Sr. Galgo está cortando el césped. Rodrigo está comiendo una manzana y Mariana está poniendo la mesa.*

1. 10:00

_____

_____

_____

_____

2. 3:00

_____

_____

_____

3. 8:00

_____

_____

_____

_____

Actividad 13

A. Read the letter that Marta wrote to "Querida Adela," an advice column in the local paper, because she was frustrated with having to help around the house.

> *Querida Adela:*
>
> *Yo soy una hija de 16 años y no tengo tiempo para ayudar en la casa. Mis padres no comprenden que yo tengo mi propia vida y que mis amigos son más importantes que los quehaceres de la casa. ¿Qué debo hacer?*
>
>   *—Hija Malcontenta*

B. Now, imagine that you are Adela and are writing a response to Marta. In the first paragraph, tell her what she must do around the house. In the second, tell her what she can do to still have fun with her friends. Use the sentences already below to help you.

> Querida Hija Malcontenta:
>
>   Es verdad que tú tienes un problema. Piensas que tu vida con tus amigos es más importante que tu vida con tu familia. Pero, hija, tú tienes responsabilidades. Arregla tu cuarto. _____
>
> _____
>
> _____
>
> _____
>
> Tienes que ser una buena hija.
>
>   Después de ayudar a tus padres, llama a tus amigos por teléfono.
>
> _____
>
> _____
>
> _____
>
> _____. Tus padres van a estar más contentos y tú vas a tener una vida mejor.
>
>   Buena suerte
>
>   *Adela*

Nombre _____ Hora _____

Fecha _____

VIDEO

Antes de ver el video

Actividad 1

In the next video, Claudia and Teresa go shopping for clothes. In order to make decisions on what they want they will sometimes make comparisons. Using the following words, make a comparative statement for each set. Follow the model.

Modelo   blusa roja / blusa amarilla

La blusa roja es más bonita que la blusa amarilla. _____

1. botas marrones / botas negras

   _____

2. una falda larga / una mini falda

   _____

3. un traje nuevo / un traje de moda (*in fashion*)

   _____

4. Claudia – 16 años / Teresa – 15 años

   _____

5. suéter que cuesta 40 dólares / suéter que cuesta 30 dólares

   _____

¿Comprendes?

Actividad 2

Identify the speaker of the following quotes by writing the name of each person on the space provided.

1. "Tienes ropa muy bonita."   _____

2. "Quiero comprar algo nuevo."   _____

3. "¿Qué tal esta tienda?"   _____

Realidades ①

Capítulo 7A

Nombre _____

Fecha _____

Hora _____

VIDEO

4. "Pues entonces, ¿esta falda y esta blusa?" _____

5. "Busco algo bonito para una fiesta." _____

6. "Bueno, hay cosas que no cuestan tanto." _____

7. "Bueno, uhm, aquí en México no llevamos esa ropa en las fiestas." _____

8. "¡... pero es mi gorra favorita!" _____

Actividad 3

Can you remember what happened in the video? Write the letter of the correct answer on the line.

1. A Teresa no le gusta la falda y el vestido; _____
   a. le quedan bien.
   b. le quedan más o menos.
   c. le quedan mal.

2. A Teresa no le gusta su ropa, pero sí tiene ropa _____
   a. bonita.
   b. fea.
   c. muy vieja.

3. Teresa quiere _____
   a. comprar algo extravagante.
   b. comprar algo nuevo.
   c. no ir a la fiesta.

Realidades 1

Capítulo 7A

Nombre _____

Fecha _____

Hora _____

VIDEO

4. Claudia quiere ver _____

    a. cuánto cuestan la falda y la blusa.

    b. si le quedan bien los jeans y la camiseta.

    c. otras cosas más bonitas.

5. Por fin las chicas deciden comprar _____

    a. unos jeans de cuatrocientos pesos con una camiseta de doscientos pesos.

    b. en otra tienda.

    c. una falda de trescientos pesos y un suéter de doscientos pesos.

Y, ¿qué más?

Actividad 4

Do you like the clothes that you have in your closet? Write one sentence about something in your closet that you do like, and why. Then write one sentence about something in your closet that you don't like, and why not. Follow the models.

Modelo 1 _Me gusta el suéter negro porque es bonito y puedo llevarlo_

cuando hace frío.

_____

_____

Modelo 2 _No me gustan los pantalones rojos porque son feos y me quedan mal._

_____

_____

Nombre _____ Hora _____

Fecha _____

AUDIO

Actividad 5

Isabel is working at a laundry (**lavandería**) in Salamanca. As the customers bring in their order, write how many clothing items each person has from each category in the appropriate boxes. Then total the order and write the amount in the blanks provided in the grid for each customer. You will hear each dialogue twice.

LAVANDERÍA DOS PASOS

(Note: € is the symbol for Euros)

	Precios	Cliente 1	Cliente 2	Cliente 3	Cliente 4	Cliente 5
Blusas	3 €					
Vestidos	6 €					
Pantalones	8 €					
Faldas	5 €					
Suéteres	5 €					
Camisas	3 €					
Jeans	7 €					
Chaquetas	9 €					
Camisetas	3 €					
	TOTAL					

Actividad 6

Listen to the following items available from one of the shopping services on TV. You might not understand all of the words, but listen for the words that you do know in order to identify which item is being discussed. Then write down the price underneath the correct picture. You will hear each set of statements twice.

_____   _____   _____   _____   _____

Nombre _____ Hora _____

Fecha _____

AUDIO

Actividad 7

Listen as friends talk about their plans for the weekend. Where are they thinking about going? What are they thinking about doing? How are they planning to dress? As you listen for these details, fill in the chart. You will hear each dialogue twice.

	¿Adónde piensa ir?	¿Qué piensa hacer?	¿Qué piensa llevar?
1. Paco			
2. Anita			
3. Ernesto			
4. Kiki			

Actividad 8

Susi is spending the summer in Ecuador, where she is living with a wonderful host family. As the summer comes to a close, she is searching for the perfect thank-you gifts for each member of the family. Listen as she talks to the sales clerk. In the chart below, write in the item that she decides to buy for each person in her new "family." You will hear this conversation twice.

Para la madre	Para el padre	Para el hijo, Luis	Para la hija, Marisol	Para el bebé

Nombre _____

Hora _____

Fecha _____

Actividad 9

What you wear can reveal secrets about your personality. Find out what type of message you send when you wear your favorite clothes and your favorite colors. As you listen to the descriptions, write down at least one word or phrase for each color personality and at least one article of clothing favored by that person. You will hear each set of statements twice.

EL COLOR	LA ROPA	LA PERSONALIDAD
Rojo		
Amarillo		
Morado		
Azul		
Anaranjado		
Marrón		
Gris		
Verde		
Negro		

Realidades 1

Capítulo 7A

Nombre _____

Hora _____

Fecha _____

WRITING

Actividad 10

Answer the following questions about clothing and shopping in complete sentences.

1. ¿Quién va mucho de compras en tu familia?

_____

2. ¿Piensas comprar ropa nueva esta estación? ¿Qué piensas comprar?

_____

_____

3. ¿Cuál prefieres, la ropa del verano o la ropa del invierno? ¿Por qué?

_____

_____

4. ¿Prefieres la ropa de tus amigos o la ropa de tus padres? ¿Por qué?

_____

_____

5. ¿Prefieres llevar ropa formal o informal?

_____

6. ¿Qué llevas normalmente para ir a la escuela?

_____

_____

_____

7. ¿Cuál es tu ropa favorita? Describe.

_____

_____

_____

Realidades 1

Capítulo 7A

Nombre _____

Hora _____

Fecha _____

WRITING

Actividad 11

Some students are thinking about what to wear for the next school dance. Look at the pictures, then write complete sentences telling what the students might be thinking. Use the verbs **pensar, querer,** or **preferir.** Follow the model.

Modelo

María piensa llevar un vestido negro al baile. También quiere llevar
unos zapatos negros. Quiere ser muy elegante.

1. _____

_____

_____

2. _____

_____

_____

3. _____

_____

_____

Realidades ❶

Capítulo 7A

Nombre _____

Hora _____

Fecha _____

WRITING

Actividad 12

Pedro works in a department store and handles customer inquiries in the clearance clothing department. The items in his department are on sale, while the items in the rest of the store are full price. Help him answer customers' questions about the merchandise by writing complete sentences that include demonstrative adjectives. Follow the model.

Modelo   ¿Cuánto cuestan los suéteres?

Estos suéteres aquí cuestan cuarenta dólares y esos allí cuestan sesenta.

1. ¿Cuánto cuesta una gorra negra?

   _____

2. ¿Cuánto cuestan los pantalones?

   _____

3. ¿Las camisas cuestan diez dólares?

   _____

4. ¿Cuánto cuesta un traje de baño?

   _____

5. ¿Los jeans cuestan mucho?

   _____

6. ¿La sudadera azul cuesta veinte dólares?

   _____

7. ¿Cuánto cuestan las botas aquí?

   _____

8. ¿Los abrigos cuestan mucho?

   _____

Realidades ❶

Capítulo 7A

Nombre _____

Fecha _____

Hora _____

WRITING

Actividad 13

You get a discount at the clothing store where you work after school, so you are going to buy presents for your friends and family there. Write complete sentences telling who you will buy gifts for and why you will choose each person's gift. Use the model to help you.

Modelo *Pienso comprar este suéter azul para mi madre porque ella prefiere la ropa del invierno.*

1. _____

_____

2. _____

_____

3. _____

_____

4. _____

_____

5. _____

_____

Realidades ①

Capítulo 7B

Nombre

Fecha

Hora

VIDEO

Antes de ver el video

Actividad 1

Where do you like to shop? With a partner, write three things you like to buy and the best place to buy them.

Cosas para comprar

Lugares donde comprarlas

_____   _____

_____   _____

_____   _____

¿Comprendes?

Actividad 2

In the video, Claudia and Manolo go many places to find a gift for Manolo's aunt. Look at the places from the video below and number them in the order in which Manolo and Claudia pass them (from beginning to end).

_____ el almacén

_____ la joyería

_____ la tienda de software

_____ la parada de autobuses

_____ el centro comercial

Realidades ❶

Capítulo 7B

Nombre _____

Hora _____

Fecha _____

VIDEO

Actividad 3

What happens when Claudia helps Manolo shop? Circle the letter of the correct answers.

1. Manolo necesita comprar un regalo para su tía porque

    a. mañana es su cumpleaños.

    b. mañana es su aniversario de bodas.

    c. mañana es su quinceañera.

2. El año pasado Manolo le compró a su tía

    a. unos aretes en la joyería.

    b. un libro en una librería.

    c. una corbata muy barata.

3. En el centro comercial, ellos ven

    a. videojuegos y software.

    b. pocas cosas en descuento.

    c. anteojos para sol, bolsos, carteras y llaveros.

4. Por fin, deciden comprar para la tía

    a. una cartera.

    b. un collar.

    c. un anillo.

5. Hay una confusión y Manolo le regala a la tía

    a. una pulsera.

    b. unos guantes.

    c. un collar de perro.

Nombre _____ Hora _____

Fecha _____

VIDEO

Y, ¿qué más?

Actividad 4

You are shopping for a birthday gift for your mother. Fill in the dialogue below with your possible responses.

DEPENDIENTE: ¿Qué desea usted?

TÚ: _____

_____

DEPENDIENTE: ¿Prefiere ver ropa, perfumes o joyas para ella?

TÚ: _____

_____

DEPENDIENTE: Aquí hay muchos artículos, pero no cuestan tanto.

TÚ: _____

_____

Realidades ①

Capítulo 7B

Nombre _____

Fecha _____

Hora _____

AUDIO

Actividad 5

Sometimes giving gifts is even more fun than receiving them! Listen as people talk about gifts they enjoy giving to their friends and family. Match the pictures below with the corresponding description you hear. Then, in the spaces next to each gift, write where the person bought the gift and what the person paid for it. You will hear each set of statements twice.

	Descripción	Lugar de compra	Precio
1.	_____	_____	_____
2.	_____	_____	_____
3.	_____	_____	_____
4.	_____	_____	_____
5.	_____	_____	_____

Actividad 6

Listen to the following mini-conversations about different kinds of stores. Circle **lógico** if the conversation makes sense and **ilógico** if it does not. You will hear each dialogue twice.

1. lógico   ilógico   6. lógico   ilógico

2. lógico   ilógico   7. lógico   ilógico

3. lógico   ilógico   8. lógico   ilógico

4. lógico   ilógico   9. lógico   ilógico

5. lógico   ilógico   10. lógico   ilógico

Nombre _____ Hora _____

Fecha _____

AUDIO

Actividad 7

Listen as Lorena shows a friend her photographs. Write a sentence describing each one as you hear Lorena describe it. You will hear each conversation twice.

1. Lorena _____ hace _____.

2. Lorena _____ hace _____.

3. Lorena _____ hace _____.

4. Lorena _____ hace _____.

5. Lorena _____ hace _____.

Actividad 8

You have been waiting in line all day at the mall, so you have overheard many conversations as you waited. See if you can match each conversation with the illustrations below and write the number of each conversation under the correct illustration. You will hear each conversation twice.

_____   _____   _____   _____

Realidades ①

Capítulo 7B

Nombre _____

Hora _____

Fecha _____

AUDIO

Actividad 9

As a special holiday service, **El Almacén Continental** is sponsoring a hotline that customers can call to get gift ideas. Listen as callers tell the store specialist what they have bought for a particular person in the past. Then listen to the specialist's suggestion for this year's gift. Use the chart below to take notes. You will hear each conversation twice.

	La personalidad y las actividades de la persona	El regalo del año pasado	¿Un regalo para este año?
1			
2			
3			
4			
5			

Nombre _____

Hora _____

Fecha _____

Actividad 10

You are talking to a friend about what you buy when you go shopping. Tell what items you usually buy in each of the specialty shops suggested by the pictures. Then, tell what other items are available at the store. Use the model to help you.

Modelo

En la zapatería, compro zapatos y botas. También es posible comprar guantes y carteras en una zapatería.

1. _____

_____

_____

2. _____

_____

_____

3. _____

_____

_____

Realidades ①

Capítulo 7B

Nombre _____

Hora _____

Fecha _____

WRITING

Actividad 11

In your Spanish class, you are asked to learn the dates of some important events in the history and culture of Spanish-speaking countries. To help you memorize these dates, write sentences telling when each event occurred. Follow the model.

Modelo Pablo Picasso / pintar su cuadro *Guernica* / 1937

Pablo Picasso pintó su cuadro Guernica en 1937.

1. Los Estados Unidos / declarar su independencia / el cuatro de julio, 1776

   _____

2. Vicente Fox / ganar la presidencia de México / 2000

   _____

3. Antonio Banderas / actuar en la película *The Mambo Kings* / 1993

   _____

4. Los jugadores argentinos / ganar la Copa Mundial (*World Cup*) / 1986

   _____

5. Yo / comprar mis primeros zapatos / ???

   _____

6. Nosotros / entrar en la clase de español / ???

   _____

7. Los Juegos Olímpicos / pasar en España / 1992

   _____

8. México / declarar su independencia / el quince de septiembre, 1810

   _____

9. Simón Bolívar / liberar a Venezuela / 1821

   _____

Realidades 1

Capítulo 7B

Nombre

Hora

Fecha

WRITING

Actividad 12

The people in your neighborhood were very busy yesterday. Write at least three sentences about what they all did based on the pictures, using at least one of these verbs: **buscar, jugar, pagar, practicar, sacar, tocar.** Follow the model.

Modelo   El Sr. Rodríguez

Ayer el Sr. Rodríguez enseñó la clase de español. La clase practicó la lección. Los estudiantes usaron las computadoras para hacer las actividades.

1. Andrés

_____

_____

2. yo

_____

_____

3. yo   mi madre

_____

_____

Realidades ①

Capítulo 7B

Nombre _____

Hora _____

Fecha _____

WRITING

4.   tú

_____

_____

_____

5.   Juana e Inés

_____

_____

_____

Actividad 13

You are writing a letter to your aunt in Mexico to tell her what you bought for your family for the holidays. In the letter, tell what you bought for each person, in what stores you found the items, and how much you paid. The letter has been started for you.

Querida Tía:

    Saludos de los Estados Unidos. Te escribo para decirte que terminé de comprar los regalos para la familia. Para _____ , compré un suéter bonito. ¡Lo encontré en el almacén por sólo veinte dólares! _____

_____

_____

_____

_____

    Bueno, nos vemos en una semana. ¡Buena suerte con las compras!

                     Un fuerte abrazo,

                     Tu sobrino(a) _____

Nombre _____ Hora _____

Fecha _____

VIDEO

Antes de ver el video

Actividad 1

You can see and learn a lot on a day trip. Make a list of four places you would like to visit for the day, and write next to each one the main attraction that you would like to see there. Follow the model.

Lugares	Cosas que ver
Modelo _Granada, España_	_La Alhambra_
_____	_____
_____	_____
_____	_____

¿Comprendes?

Actividad 2

Raúl, Gloria, and Tomás went on a day trip to San José and Sarapiquí Park. Under each heading, write the things that they saw in San José and the things that they saw in Sarapiquí Park.

Ministerio de Cultura	mono	Parque España	Catarata La Paz
Gran Terminal del Caribe	palma	bosque lluvioso	Teatro Nacional

San José	Parque Sarapiquí
_____	_____
_____	_____
_____	_____
_____	_____

Realidades ❶

Capítulo 8A

Nombre _____

Hora _____

Fecha _____

VIDEO

Actividad 3

Based on the video story that you just watched, circle the most appropriate word to complete each statement.

1. Raúl, Gloria y Tomás salieron de la casa muy (tarde / temprano) para ir al parque Sarapiquí.

2. Para ir al parque ellos tomaron el (autobús / avión).

3. El viaje dura (una hora y media / dos horas), porque el parque está a 82 (kilómetros / millas) de San José.

4. En el parque (hace mucho calor / no hace ni frío ni calor) pero llueve mucho.

5. Raúl compra los (libros / boletos) en la Estación Biológica La Selva y cuestan 3,600 (pesos / colones).

6. Tomás tiene la (mochila / cámara) y el (boleto / mapa) y está listo para explorar el parque.

7. Ellos tienen mucho cuidado cuando caminan, pues las raíces de los árboles son muy (grandes / interesantes).

8. Gloria le dice a Tomás: "Hay más de cuatrocientas especies de (monos / aves) en el parque."

9. Ellos tienen problemas al (sacar las fotos / regresar a casa). Pero Tomás (quiere / no quiere) continuar.

10. Raúl dice: "Fue un día (interesante / desastre) pero un poco (difícil / aburrido) para Tomás."

Nombre _____   Hora _____

Fecha _____

VIDEO

Y, ¿qué más?

Actividad 4

Based on what you learned in the video, imagine that you took a field trip to Costa Rica. Your best friend is curious about your trip. Answer your friend's questions below.

1. —¿Cómo es el parque Sarapiquí?

   —_____

2. —¿Sacaste fotos del parque?

   —_____

3. —¿Qué fue lo que más te gustó?

   —_____

4. —¿Qué fue lo que menos te gustó?

   —_____

5. —¿Cuál es la comida típica de Costa Rica?

   —_____

Realidades ❶

Capítulo 8A

Nombre _____

Fecha _____

Hora _____

AUDIO

Actividad 5

You call a toll-free telephone number in order to qualify for the popular radio game show, **"Palabras Secretas"** (*Secret Words*). Your challenge is to guess each secret word within ten seconds. Listen to the clues and try to guess the word as the clock is ticking. You must write your answer down before the buzzer in order to be ready for the next one. You will hear each set of statements twice.

1. _____   5. _____

2. _____   6. _____

3. _____   7. _____

4. _____   8. _____

Actividad 6

Listen as a husband and wife talk to a travel agent about their upcoming vacation. Where would each like to go? What type of things would each like to do? Most importantly, do they agree on what is the ideal trip? As you listen, write as much information as you can in each person's travel profile in the chart below. Can you think of a place they could go where both of them would be happy? You will hear this conversation twice.

	EL SEÑOR	LA SEÑORA
¿Adónde le gustaría ir?		
¿Por qué le gustaría ir a ese lugar?		
Cuando va de vacaciones, ¿qué le gustaría hacer?	1. 2.	1. 2.
¿Qué le gustaría ver?	1. 2.	1. 2.
¿Cómo le gustaría viajar?		
¿Adónde deben ir?		

Realidades ❶

Capítulo 8A

Nombre _____

Fecha _____

Hora _____

AUDIO

Actividad 7

Listen as mothers call their teenaged sons and daughters on their cell phones to see if they have done what they were asked to do. Based on what each teenager says, categorize the answers in the chart. You will hear each conversation twice.

	1	2	3	4	5	6	7	8	9	10
Teen did what the parent asked him or her to do.										
Teen is in the middle of doing what the parent asked him or her to do.										
Teen says he/she is going to do what the parent asked him/her to do.										

Actividad 8

Your Spanish teacher has asked the students in your class to survey each other about a topic of interest. In order to give you a model to follow, your teacher will play a recording of part of a student's survey from last year. Listen to the student's questions, and fill in his survey form. You will hear each conversation twice.

	¿EL LUGAR?
1. Marco	
2. Patricia	
3. Chucho	
4. Rita	
5. Margarita	

Realidades ❶

Capítulo 8A

Nombre _____

Hora _____

Fecha _____

AUDIO

Actividad 9

Everyone loves a superhero, and the listeners of this Hispanic radio station are no exception. Listen to today's episode of "Super Tigre," as the hero helps his friends try to locate the evil Rona Robles! Super Tigre tracks Rona Robles down by asking people when they last saw her and where she went. Keep track of what the people said by filling in the chart. You will hear each conversation twice.

	¿Dónde la vio?	¿A qué hora la vio?	¿Qué hizo ella? (What did she do?)	¿Adónde fue ella?
1				
2				
3				
4				
5				

Where did Super Tigre finally find Rona Robles? _____

Nombre _____

Hora _____

Fecha _____

WRITING

Actividad 10

Answer the following questions in complete sentences.

1. ¿Te gusta ir de viaje? ¿Te gustaría más ir de vacaciones al campo o a una ciudad?

   _____

   _____

2. ¿Visitaste algún parque nacional en el pasado? ¿Cuál(es)? Si no, ¿te gustaría visitar

   un parque nacional? _____

   _____

3. ¿Vives cerca de un lago? ¿Cómo se llama? ¿Te gusta nadar? ¿Pasear en bote?

   _____

   _____

4. ¿Te gusta ir al mar? ¿Qué te gusta hacer allí? Si no, ¿por qué no? _____

   _____

   _____

5. ¿Montaste a caballo alguna vez? ¿Te gustó o no? Si no, ¿te gustaría montar a caballo?

   _____

   _____

6. Describe tu lugar favorito para vivir. ¿Está cerca de un lago? ¿Cerca o lejos de
   la ciudad? ¿Hay montañas / museos / parques / un mar cerca de tu casa ideal?

   _____

   _____

   _____

   _____

Realidades **1**

Capítulo 8A

Nombre _____

Hora _____

Fecha _____

WRITING

Actividad 11

You and your friends are talking about what you did over the weekend. Write complete sentences based on the illustrations to tell what the following people did. Follow the model.

Modelo   Pablo *vio una película* _____.

1.   Mariela y su madre _____.

2.   Nosotros _____.

3.   Yo _____.

4.   Roberto _____.

5.   Norma _____.

6.   Tú _____.

7.   Ignacio e Isabel _____.

Actividad 12

You and your friends were very busy yesterday. Tell all the places where each person went using the illustrations as clues. Follow the model.

Modelo Melisa y su padre *fueron de compras.*
Después, fueron al cine. _____

1. David _____

_____

_____

2. Yo _____

_____

_____

3. Nosotros _____

_____

_____

4. Raquel y Tito _____

_____

_____

Actividad 13

A. Write two sentences telling what places you visited the last time you went on vacation. You can write about your ideal vacation if you would prefer. Follow the model.

Modelo   *Fui al parque de diversiones.*

1. _____

2. _____

B. Write two sentences telling about people you saw when you were on vacation.

Modelo   *Vi a mi abuela.*

1. _____

2. _____

C. Now, complete the letter below to your friend. Use your sentences from Part A and Part B and additional details to tell him or her about your vacation.

Querido(a) _____ :

¡Hola! ¿Cómo estás? Gracias por tu carta de la semana pasada. Te voy a contar un poco de nuestras vacaciones del mes pasado. _____

_____

_____

_____

Y cuando fuimos a otro lugar, vimos _____

_____

_____

_____

_____

_____

Un abrazo,

_____

Realidades ❶

Capítulo 8B

Nombre _____

Hora _____

Fecha _____

VIDEO

Antes de ver el video

Actividad 1

There are lots of things you can do to make the world a better place. Under each category, write two things that you would like to do to help.

Cómo ayudar...

en mi comunidad _____

_____

con el ambiente _____

_____

¿Comprendes?

Actividad 2

In the video, the friends talk about how to help in their communities through volunteer work. Circle the letter of the appropriate answer for each question.

1. Gloria y Raúl trabajan como voluntarios en

    a. un centro de ancianos.

    b. Casa Latina.

    c. el Hospital Nacional de Niños.

2. Tomás va al hospital porque

    a. está enfermo.

    b. a él le encanta el trabajo voluntario.

    c. tiene que llevar ropa para los niños.

3. Gloria dice: "Trabajar con los niños en el hospital es

    a. muy aburrido."

    b. una experiencia inolvidable."

    c. un trabajo que no me gusta."

4. En su comunidad, Tomás trabaja como voluntario

    a. dando comida a los pobres.

    b. enseñando a leer a los ancianos.

    c. recogiendo ropa usada para los pobres.

5. Ellos también cuidan el ambiente reciclando

    a. aluminio y periódicos.

    b. papel, plástico y vidrio.

    c. papel, vidrio y aluminio.

Actividad 3

Fill in the blanks from the box below to complete the story.

reciclar	importante	libros	pasado
ancianos	comunidad	voluntarios	difícil
lava	simpáticos	trabajo	

En el Hospital Nacional de Niños, Tomás y Gloria trabajan como (1) _____ .

Allí ellos cantan, leen (2) _____ y juegan con los niños. A veces los niños

están muy enfermos y es (3) _____ , pero los niños son muy

(4) _____ . Raúl trabajó en un centro de (5) _____ el año (6)

_____ . Allí les ayudó con la comida y hablando con ellos.

    Tomás también trabaja en su (7) _____ ; él ayuda a recoger ropa usada.

Después la separa, la (8) _____ y luego la da a la gente pobre del barrio.

Es mucho (9) _____ , pero le gusta.

    Todos ellos ayudan a (10) _____ el papel y las botellas pues, piensan que

reciclar y conservar es muy (11) _____ .

Nombre _____

Hora _____

Fecha _____

VIDEO

Y, ¿qué más?

Actividad 4

Now that you have seen Tomás, Gloria, and Raúl working in various ways to help others, think about the organizations that make it possible for them to do this work. Imagine that you work with one of the organizations listed below, and write a paragraph about your experiences. Use the model to help you.

el Hospital Nacional de Niños

un centro de ancianos

el club Casa Latina

Modelo *Me gusta trabajar en el centro de ancianos. Les ayudo con la comida y paso tiempo escuchando sus cuentos.*

_____

_____

_____

_____

_____

_____

Realidades 1

Capítulo 8B

Nombre _____

Hora _____

Fecha _____

AUDIO

Actividad 5

Listen as Sra. Muñoz, the Spanish Club sponsor, asks several students what they did last weekend. If a student's actions had a positive impact on their community, place a check mark in the corresponding box or boxes. If a student's actions had no positive effect on their community, place an *X* in the corresponding box or boxes. You will hear each conversation twice.

	Javier	Ana	José	Celi	Pablo	Laura	Sra. Muñoz
enseñar a los niños a leer							
reciclar la basura de las calles							
jugar al fútbol con amigos							
recoger y lavar la ropa usada para la gente pobre							
trabajar en un centro para ancianos							
traer juguetes a los niños que están en el hospital							
trabajar en un restaurante del centro comercial							

Actividad 6

Listen as people talk about what they did last Saturday. Did they do volunteer work in the community or did they earn spending money for themselves? Place a check mark in the correct box on the grid. You will hear each set of statements twice.

	1	2	3	4	5	6	7	8
(hand)								
(money)								

Actividad 7

Listen as our leaders, friends, and family give advice to teenagers about what we must do to serve our communities. Use the grid below to take notes as you listen. Then, use your notes to complete the sentences below. For example, you might write **"El vicepresidente de los Estados Unidos *dice que hay que reciclar la basura de las calles.*"** In the last sentence, complete a statement about your personal suggestion for others. You will hear each set of statements twice.

¿Quién(es) lo dice(n)?	¿Qué dice(n)?
1. El presidente de los Estados Unidos	
2. Mis padres	
3. Los médicos del hospital	
4. Mis profesores	
5. Mis amigos y yo	

1. El presidente de los Estados Unidos _____

_____ .

2. Los padres _____

_____ .

3. Los médicos _____

_____ .

4. Los profesores _____

_____ .

5. Mis amigos _____

_____ .

6. Yo

_____

_____ .

Realidades 1

Capítulo 8B

Nombre _____

Fecha _____

Hora _____

AUDIO

Actividad 8

As you hear each of the following statements, imagine whom the speaker might be addressing. Choose from the list of people, and write the number of the statement on the corresponding blank. You will hear each set of statements twice.

_____ al médico

_____ a la policía

_____ al camarero

_____ a la profesora de español

_____ a sus padres

_____ a un niño de cinco años

_____ a un voluntario del hospital

_____ a una persona que trabaja en el zoológico

Actividad 9

Abuela Consuelo always has her grandchildren over for the holidays. She wants to know what they have done over the past year. They also remind her what she gave them last year as a gift. Use the grid to help keep track of each grandchild's story. You will hear each conversation twice.

	¿Qué hizo el niño el año pasado?	¿Qué le dio la abuela al niño el año pasado?
Marta		
Jorge		
Sara		
Miguel		
Angélica		

Nombre _____

Hora _____

Fecha _____

Actividad 10

Answer the following questions in complete sentences.

1. ¿Hay lugares para hacer trabajo voluntario en tu comunidad?

_____

¿Qué hacen allí? _____

_____

2. ¿Te gustaría trabajar como voluntario en:

un hospital? ¿Por qué? _____

_____

un centro para personas pobres? ¿Por qué? _____

_____

un centro para ancianos? ¿Por qué? _____

_____

3. ¿Tu familia recicla? _____

¿Qué reciclan Uds.? _____

_____

¿Por qué es importante reciclar? _____

_____

¿Te gustaría ayudar con el reciclaje en tu comunidad? ____

_____

Actividad 11

All of the following people were asked to speak on a subject. You are reporting on what everyone says. Use each item only once. Follow the model.

yo	el trabajo voluntario
nosotros	el campamento de deportes
Sra. Ayala	el reciclaje
Dr. Riviera	el fútbol
tú	el teatro
Paco	la ropa
José y María	la salud
Alicia y yo	los quehaceres

Modelo   *La señora Ayala dice que el trabajo voluntario es una*
experiencia inolvidable.

1. _____

2. _____

3. _____

4. _____

5. _____

6. _____

7. _____

Realidades ①

Capítulo 8B

Nombre _____

Fecha _____

Hora _____

WRITING

Actividad 12

You are finding out what everyone's plans are for the weekend. Choose a verb and a direct object pronoun from the banks and write a sentence about weekend plans for each subject given. Use each verb only once. Follow the model.

ayudar	dar	decir	enseñar	escribir
hacer	invitar	leer	llevar	traer

me	te	le	nos	les

Modelo _Miguel y Elena nos invitan a su fiesta._

1. Mis padres _____.

2. Yo _____.

3. Uds. _____.

4. Nuestra profesora de español _____.

5. El presidente _____.

6. Rafael y Gabriel _____.

7. Tu mejor amigo _____.

8. El Sr. Fuentes _____.

9. La Sra. Allende _____.

10. Tú _____.

WRITING

Actividad 13

Last week, your Spanish class did some volunteer work at the local nursing home. Read the thank you letter from the residents, then write a paragraph explaining at least four things that you and your classmates did for them. Remember to use the preterite tense and indirect object pronouns where necessary. Follow the model.

Queridos muchachos:

Les escribimos para decirles "gracias" por su generosa visita de la semana pasada.
A la señora Blanco le gustó el libro de poesía que Uds. le regalaron. Todos lo pasamos
bien. Nos gustó especialmente la canción "Feliz Navidad" que cantó Luisita. El señor
Marcos todavía habla de los pasteles que las chicas le trajeron. Y nuestro jardín está
más bonito que nunca, después de todo su trabajo. En fin, mil gracias de parte de
todos aquí en Pinos Sombreados. Esperamos verles pronto.

Fuertes abrazos,

Los residentes

Modelo   *Nosotros visitamos a los residentes de Pinos Sombreados la semana pasada.*

_____

_____

_____

_____

_____

_____

_____

_____

Nombre _____

Hora _____

Fecha _____

VIDEO

Antes de ver el video

Actividad 1

In the second column, write the title of a movie or a television program that is associated with the category in the first column. The first one is done for you.

Programa o película	Nombre del programa o película
telenovelas	"Days of Our Lives"
noticias	
programas de entrevistas	
programas de la vida real	
películas de ciencia ficción	
programas de concurso	
programas educativos	
programas de deportes	
comedias	
dibujos animados	
películas románticas	
programas infantiles	

Nombre _____ Hora _____

Fecha _____

VIDEO

¿Comprendes?

Actividad 2

Look at the pictures and write what type of program each one is. Then, write the name of the character in the video who likes this type of program.

	CATEGORY	CHARACTER'S NAME
1.	_____	_____
2.	_____	_____
3.	_____	_____
4.	_____	_____
5.	_____	_____

Actividad 3

Using complete sentences, answer the following questions about what happens in the video.

1. ¿Quién tiene el mando a distancia primero?

   _____

2. ¿Qué piensa Ana de la telenovela "El amor es loco"?

   _____

Realidades 1

Capítulo 9A

Nombre _____

Fecha _____

Hora _____

VIDEO

3. ¿A quiénes les encantan las telenovelas?

_____

4. ¿Qué piensa Ignacio de los programas de la vida real?

_____

5. ¿Qué piensa Jorgito de escuchar música en el cuarto de su hermana?

_____

6. ¿Qué deciden hacer los amigos al final?

_____

7. ¿Qué quiere ver Elena en el cine? ¿Están de acuerdo Ignacio y Javier?

_____

Y, ¿qué más?

Actividad 4

What kind of TV programs do you like? What type of movies do you enjoy watching? Explain your preferences. Follow the model.

Modelo

A mí me gustan mucho los programas de concursos; son muy divertidos porque puedes jugarlos en casa con tu familia o amigos. Mi hermano prefiere los deportes; siempre quiere el mando a distancia para ver los juegos. Cuando voy al cine prefiero ver comedias, pues las películas románticas son aburridas.

_____

_____

_____

_____

Nombre _____

Hora _____

Fecha _____

AUDIO

Actividad 5

Your friend is reading you the television line-up for a local television station. After listening to each program description, fill in on the grid what day or days the program is shown, what time it is shown, and what type of program it is. You will hear each set of statements twice.

	Día(s)	Hora	Clase de programa
"Mi computadora"			
"La detective Morales"			
"Cine en su sofá"			
"Las aventuras del Gato Félix"			
"Cara a cara"			
"Lo mejor del béisbol"			
"Marisol"			
"Festival"			
"Treinta minutos"			
"Las Américas"			

Actividad 6

Listen as people in a video rental store talk about what kind of movie they want to rent. After listening to each conversation, put the letter of the type of film they agree on in the space provided. You will hear each conversation twice.

1. _____

2. _____

3. _____

4. _____

5. _____

6. _____

7. _____

A. una película policíaca

B. una comedia

C. un drama

D. una película de ciencia ficción

E. una película romántica

F. una película de horror

G. una película de dibujos animados

Nombre _____ Hora _____

Fecha _____

Actividad 7

Listen to a film critic interviewing five people on opening night of the movie *Marruecos*. After listening to each person's interview, circle the number of stars that closely matches the person's opinion of the movie, from a low rating of one star to a high rating of four. After noting all of the opinions, give the movie an overall rating of one to four stars, and give a reason for your answer. You will hear each conversation twice.

	No le gustó nada	Le gustó más o menos	Le gustó mucho	Le encantó
1.	[★]	[★★]	[★★★]	[★★★★]
2.	[★]	[★★]	[★★★]	[★★★★]
3.	[★]	[★★]	[★★★]	[★★★★]
4.	[★]	[★★]	[★★★]	[★★★★]
5.	[★]	[★★]	[★★★]	[★★★★]

¿Cuántas estrellas para *Marruecos*? ¿Por qué? _____

Actividad 8

Listen as two friends talk on the phone about what they just saw on TV. Do they seem to like the same type of programs? As you listen to their conversation, fill in the Venn diagram, indicating: 1) which programs only Alicia likes; 2) which programs both Alicia and Laura like; and 3) which programs only Laura likes. You will hear this conversation twice.

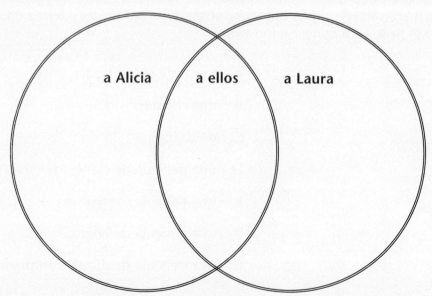

a Alicia   a ellos   a Laura

Realidades ❶

Capítulo 9A

Nombre _____

Hora _____

Fecha _____

AUDIO

Actividad 9

Listen as a television critic reviews some of the new shows of the season. As you listen, determine which shows he likes and dislikes, and why. Fill in the chart. You will hear each paragraph twice.

	Le gusta...	¿Por qué le gusta?	No le gusta...	¿Por qué no le gusta?
1				
2				
3				
4				
5				

Actividad 10

Answer the following questions about movies and television.

1. ¿Te gusta ir al cine?

   _____

2. ¿Prefieres los dramas o las comedias? ¿Por qué? _____

   _____

   _____

3. ¿Cómo se llama tu película favorita? ¿Qué clase de película es?

   _____

   _____

4. ¿Te gustan las películas policíacas? ¿Por qué? _____

   _____

5. ¿Te gusta más ver le tele o leer? ¿Por qué? _____

   _____

   _____

6. ¿Qué clase de programas prefieres? ¿Por qué? _____

   _____

   _____

7. ¿Cuántos canales de televisión puedes ver en casa? _____

   ¿Cuál es tu canal favorito? _____

   ¿Por qué? _____

8. ¿Tienes un programa favorito? ¿Cómo se llama? _____

   _____

WRITING

Actividad 11

Your school newspaper printed a picture of the preparations for the Cinco de Mayo party at your school. Describe the photo using a form of **acabar de** + infinitive to tell what everyone just finished doing before the picture was taken.

| **Modelo** | *Horacio Ibáñez acaba de sacar la foto.* _____ |

1. Isabel _____

_____

2. Julia y Ramón _____

_____

3. Yo _____

_____

4. La señora Lemaños _____

_____

5. Ana _____

_____

Realidades 1

Capítulo 9A

Nombre _____

Fecha _____

Hora _____

WRITING

Actividad 12

You and your friends are talking about movies. Tell about people's preferences by choosing a subject from the first column and matching it with words from the other two columns to make complete sentences. Use each subject only once, but words from the other columns can be used more than once. Follow the model.

nosotros	gustar	las películas románticas
mis padres	encantar	las película de horror
mí	aburrir	las películas policíacas
ti	interesar	las comedias
los profesores	disgustar	los dramas
mis amigas		
mi abuelo		

Modelo *A mí me encantan las películas románticas.* _____

1. _____

2. _____

3. _____

4. _____

5. _____

6. _____

Realidades 1

Capítulo 9A

Nombre _____

Hora _____

Fecha _____

WRITING

Actividad 13

You are writing your new Spanish-speaking pen pal an e-mail about American television. First tell him about a program that you just saw. What type of show was it? Did you like it? Was it interesting? Then, tell him about two other types of TV shows that are popular in America. Make sure to tell him your opinion of these types of shows, and what some other people you know think about them.

Fecha: 20 de abril

Tema: La televisión

Querido Pancho:

   ¡Hola! ¿Cómo estás? Acabo de terminar de ver el programa _____

_____ . A mí _____

_____

_____

_____

   En los Estados Unidos, la gente ve mucho la tele. _____

_____

_____

_____

_____

¡Te escribo pronto!

                                                            Un abrazo,

                                                    _____

Realidades ①

Capítulo 9B

Nombre _____

Hora _____

Fecha _____

VIDEO

Antes de ver el video

Actividad 1

How do you communicate with your friends from far away? Using the word bank below, write two sentences about how you might stay in touch with long distance friends.

cámara digital	correo electrónico
ordenador / computadora	cibercafé
navegar en la Red	página Web
información	salones de chat
dirección electrónica	foto digital

_____

_____

_____

_____

¿Comprendes?

Actividad 2

Javier is becoming accustomed to living in Spain, but he has a lot to learn about technology. What does Ana teach him? Write **cierto** (*true*) or **falso** (*false*) next to each statement.

1. Javier conoce muy bien las cámaras digitales. _____

2. Él va a enviar una tarjeta a su amigo Esteban. _____

3. Javier le saca una foto de Ana y le gusta la cámara. _____

4. Él piensa que no es muy complicada la cámara digital. _____

5. Ana lo lleva a un cibercafé, para ordenar un café. _____

6. Empiezan a navegar en la Red. _____

7. Ana busca su página Web, pero Javier no la quiere ver. _____

8. No hay mucha información en la Red. _____

9. Pueden visitar los salones de chat, pero
   prefieren escribirle un correo electrónico a Esteban. _____

10. Esteban ve la foto digital de su amigo y piensa que está triste. _____

Actividad 3

Complete the sentences below with information from the video.

1. Javier va a enviar _____ a su amigo Esteban.

2. Ana saca muchas fotos con su _____ .

3. A Javier le gusta la cámara de Ana porque no es muy _____ .

4. Ana y Javier van a un _____ para escribirle a Esteban por _____ electrónico.

5. Según Ana, el ordenador _____ para mucho.

6. Javier quiere saber qué tal fue el _____ de Cristina.

Realidades 1

Capítulo 9B

Nombre _____

Hora _____

Fecha _____

VIDEO

Y, ¿qué más?

Actividad 4

You heard Ana and Javier talk about the many ways they use computers. Write a paragraph describing your two favorite ways to use a computer. Use the model to give you an idea of how to start.

Modelo   *En mi casa todos usan la computadora. Para mí el uso más importante es...*

_____

_____

_____

_____

_____

_____

_____

Realidades 1

Capítulo 9B

Nombre _____

Fecha _____

Hora _____

AUDIO

Actividad 5

While navigating a new Web site, two friends click on a link to a self-quiz to find out if they are **CiberAdictos.** Based on their discussion of each question, write in the chart below whether you think they answered **sí** or **no**. According to the Web site, a score of more than six **sí** answers determines that you are a **CiberAdicto.** You will hear each set of statements twice.

	1	2	3	4	5	6	7	8	¿Es CiberAdicto?
Rafael									
Miguel									

Actividad 6

Víctor has studied for the first quiz in his beginning technology class. As the teacher reads each statement, he is to answer **falso** or **cierto**. Listen to the statements and write the answers in the boxes, and take the quiz too. Would you be able to score 100%? You will hear each statement twice.

1	2	3	4	5	6	7	8	9	10

Actividad 7

Listen to the following conversations that you overhear while sitting at a table in the Café Mariposa. After listening to what each person is saying, write what they asked for in the first column and what they were served in the second column. You will hear each statement twice.

Persona	Comida pedida	Comida servida
1. Señor Cruz		
2. Señora Vargas		
3. Señor Ávila		
4. Marcelo y Daniele		
5. Señor Urbina		
6. Señora Campos		
7. Señora Suerte		

Nombre _____

Hora _____

Fecha _____

Actividad 8

Listen as teenagers talk to each other about what they need to learn how to do. The second teenager is always able to suggest someone whom the first teenager should ask for help. Match the person who is suggested to the correct picture. You will hear each set of statements twice.

_____   _____   _____

_____   _____   _____

Actividad 9

Listen as two people discuss how the computer and the Internet have changed our lives. As you listen, organize their points into two columns by summarizing what they say. You will hear each set of statements twice.

Antes de la computadora y la Red	Después de la computadora y la Red
1. _____	_____
2. _____	_____
3. _____	_____
4. _____	_____

Realidades 1

Capítulo 9B

Nombre _____

Fecha _____

Hora _____

WRITING

Actividad 10

Read the following ad about a computer of the future. Then, answer the questions below.

CEREBRADOR: ¡EL FUTURO AHORA!

¿Está cansado de ver las computadoras del futuro en una película o de leer sobre ellas en una novela? ¿Quiere el futuro ahora? ¡Pues **Cerebrador** lo tiene!

♦ La información, los gráficos, la música en la Red...
  ¡todo sin límite!

♦ Grabar un disco, escribir un informe, navegar en la Red...
  ¡sólo hay que pensarlo y se logra en poco tiempo!

♦ ¿Tiene problemas de conexión o detesta sentarse a usar la computadora?
  Sólo necesita **Cerebrador** *y dos metros de espacio para poder ver todo en la pantalla: documentos, correo electrónico, su página Web, etc. Conecte a su propia cabeza.*

Con **Cerebrador** puede sacar fotos con una minicámara digital y crear diapositivas con ellas.

Llame ahora para pedir este fenómeno.

---

1. ¿Cómo se llama la computadora del anuncio?

_____

2. ¿Qué dice el anuncio que Ud. puede hacer con esta computadora?

_____

_____

_____

3. ¿Qué necesita para usar una computadora? ¿Es una computadora portátil?

_____

_____

_____

4. ¿Cree Ud. que es posible comprar una computadora como ésta? ¿Por qué?

_____

_____

_____

_____

Nombre _____

Hora _____

Fecha _____

WRITING

Actividad 11

Your favorite restaurant has great food, but the wait staff is always messing up the orders. Using the pictures as clues and the correct forms of the verbs **pedir** and **servir**, write what happens when the following people order their meals. Follow the model and remember to use the proper indirect object pronouns in your sentences.

Modelo   Yo   El camarero

Yo pido pescado pero el camarero me sirve pollo. _____

1.   Tú   Ellos

_____

2.   Nosotros   La camarera

_____

3.   María   Uds.

_____

4.   Ellos   Nosotros

_____

5.   Ramón y Yo   Los camareros

_____

Realidades ❶

Capítulo 9B

Nombre _____

Fecha _____

Hora _____

WRITING

Actividad 12

Answer the following questions in 2–3 complete sentences using the verbs **saber** and/or **conocer**.

1. ¿Eres talentoso(a)? ¿Qué sabes hacer? ¿Tienes unos amigos muy talentosos? ¿Qué saben hacer ellos?

   _____

   _____

   _____

   _____

2. ¿Conoces a alguna persona famosa? ¿Quién? ¿Cómo es? ¿Alguien más en tu familia conoce a una persona famosa?

   _____

   _____

   _____

   _____

3. ¿Qué ciudades o países conocen tú y tu familia? ¿Cuándo los visitaste? ¿Qué lugares conocen tus amigos?

   _____

   _____

   _____

   _____

4. ¿Qué sabes de la geografía de Latinoamérica? (¿Sabes cuál es la capital de Uruguay? ¿Sabes cuántos países hay en Sudamérica?)

   _____

   _____

   _____

   _____

Realidades **1**

Nombre _____

Hora _____

Capítulo 9B

Fecha _____

WRITING

Actividad 13

Describe the **cibercafé** below. First, tell three things that you can do there. Next, tell three items that they serve at the café, using the verb **servir** and the food items in the picture. Finally, tell what you can do if you need assistance at the **cibercafé.** Use the verb **pedir,** and the verbs **saber** and **conocer** to discuss how knowledgeable the staff is (**Ellos saben ayudar…/ Ellos conocen bien la Red…**).

Ud. puede _____

_____

_____

_____

Allí ellos _____

_____

_____

_____

_____

_____

_____

_____

_____

_____

Song Lyrics

These are the lyrics for the songs that appear on the Canciones CD.

Track 01

UNO DE ENERO

Uno de enero, dos de febrero,
tres de marzo, cuatro de abril,
cinco de mayo, seis de junio,
siete de julio, San Fermín.

Uno de enero, dos de febrero,
tres de marzo, cuatro de abril,
cinco de mayo, seis de junio,
siete de julio, San Fermín.

A Pamplona hemos de ir,
con una media, con una media.
A Pamplona hemos de ir,
con una media y un calcetín.

Track 02

LA MARIPOSA

Vamos todos a cantar,
vamos todos a bailar
la morenada.

Vamos todos a cantar,
vamos todos a bailar
la morenada.

Con los tacos,
con las manos.
¡Viva la fiesta!

Con los tacos,
con las manos.
¡Viva la fiesta!

Track 03

ERES TÚ

Como una promesa eres tú, eres tú
como una mañana de verano;
como una sonrisa eres tú, eres tú;
así, así eres tú.

Toda mi esperanza eres tú, eres tú,
como lluvia fresca en mis manos;
como fuerte brisa eres tú, eres tú
así, así eres tú.

[estribillo]
Eres tú como el agua de mi fuente;
eres tú el fuego de mi hogar.
Eres tú como el fuego de mi hoguera;
eres tú el trigo de mi pan.

Como mi poema eres tú, eres tú;
como una guitarra en la noche.
Todo mi horizonte eres tú, eres tú;
así, así eres tú.

Eres tú como el agua de mi fuente;
eres tú el fuego de mi hogar.
Algo así eres tú;
algo así como el fuego de mi hoguera.
Algo así eres tú;
Mi vida, algo, algo así eres tú.

Eres tú como el fuego de mi hoguera;
eres tú el trigo de mi pan.
Algo así eres tú;
algo así como el fuego de mi hoguera.
Algo así eres tú;

Track 04

CIELITO LINDO

[estribillo]
¡Ay, ay, ay, ay!
Canta y no llores,
porque cantando se alegran,
cielito lindo, los corazones.

De la sierra morena,
cielito lindo, vienen bajando;
un par de ojitos negros,
cielito lindo, de contrabando.

¡Ay, ay, ay, ay!
Canta y no llores,
porque cantando se alegran,
cielito lindo, los corazones.

Una flecha en el aire,
cielito lindo, lanzó Cupido,

y como fue jugando,
cielito lindo, yo fui el herido.

¡Ay, ay, ay, ay!
Canta y no llores,
porque cantando se alegran,
cielito lindo, los corazones.

Pájaro que abandona,
cielito lindo, su primer nido,
si lo encuentra ocupado,
cielito lindo, ¡bien merecido!

¡Ay, ay, ay, ay!
Canta y no llores,
porque cantando se alegran,
cielito lindo, los corazones.

Track 05

LA CUCARACHA

[estribillo]
La cucaracha, la cucaracha,
ya no quiere caminar,
porque no tiene, porque le falta
dinero para gastar.

La cucaracha, la cucaracha,
ya no quiere caminar,
porque no tiene, porque le falta
dinero para gastar.

Una cucaracha pinta
le dijo a una colorada:
Vámonos para mi tierra
a pasar la temporada.

Una cucaracha pinta
le dijo a una colorada:
Vámonos para mi tierra
a pasar la temporada.

La cucaracha, la cucaracha,
ya no quiere caminar,
porque no tiene, porque le falta
dinero para gastar.

Todas las muchachas tienen
en los ojos dos estrellas,
pero las mexicanitas
de seguro son más bellas.

Todas las muchachas tienen
en los ojos dos estrellas,
pero las mexicanitas
de seguro son más bellas.

La cucaracha, la cucaracha,
ya no quiere caminar,
porque no tiene, porque le falta
dinero para gastar.

Una cosa me da risa,
Pancho Villa sin camisa,
ya se van los carrancistas,
porque vienen los villistas.

Una cosa me da risa,
Pancho Villa sin camisa,
ya se van los carrancistas,
porque vienen los villistas.

La cucaracha, la cucaracha,
ya no quiere caminar,
porque no tiene, porque le falta
dinero para gastar.

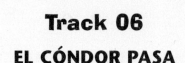

Track 06

EL CÓNDOR PASA

Al cóndor de los Andes despertó
una luz,
una luz,
de un bello amanecer, amanecer.

Sus alas en lo alto extendió
y bajó,
y bajó,
al dulce manantial, para beber.

La nieve de las cumbres brilla ya
bajo el sol, el día y la luz.
La nieve de las cumbres brilla ya
bajo el sol, el día y la luz,
del bello amanecer, amanecer.

Al cóndor de los Andes despertó
una luz,
una luz,
de un bello amanecer, amanecer.

Sus alas en lo alto extendió
y bajó,
y bajó,
al dulce manantial, para beber.

La nieve de las cumbres brilla ya
bajo el sol, el día y la luz.
La nieve de las cumbres brilla ya
bajo el sol, el día y la luz,
del bello amanecer, amanecer.

Track 07

LOS POLLOS DE MI CAZUELA

Los pollos de mi cazuela
no son para mí comer,
que son para la viudita
que los sabe componer.

Se les echa ajo y cebolla
y una hojita de laurel,
y se sacan de la cazuela
cuando se vayan a comer.

Track 08

LA BAMBA

Para bailar la bamba, para bailar la bamba
se necesita una poca de gracia,
una poca de gracia y otra cosita
y arriba y arriba,
y arriba y arriba y arriba iré,
yo no soy marinero, yo no soy marinero,
por ti seré, por ti seré, por ti seré.

Bamba, bamba...

Una vez que te dije, una vez que te dije
que eras bonita, se te puso la cara,
se te puso la cara coloradita
y arriba y arriba,
y arriba y arriba y arriba iré,
yo no soy marinero, yo no soy marinero,
soy capitán, soy capitán, soy capitán.

Bamba, bamba...

Para subir al cielo, para subir al cielo
se necesita una escalera grande,
una escalera grande y otra chiquita
y arriba y arriba,
y arriba y arriba y arriba iré,
yo no soy marinero, yo no soy marinero,
por ti seré, por ti seré, por ti seré.

Bamba, bamba...

Track 09

HIMNO DEL ATHLETIC DE BILBAO

Tiene Bilbao un gran tesoro
que adora y mima con gran pasión.
Su club de fútbol
de bella historia,
lleno de gloria,
mil veces campeón.

Athletic, Athletic club
de limpia tradición,
ninguno más que tú
lleva mejor blasón.

Del fútbol eres rey,
te llaman el león
y la afición el rey
del fútbol español.

Cantemos pues los bilbainitos,
a nuestro club con gran amor,
para animarle con nuestro himno,
el canto digno del Alirón.

¡Alirón! ¡Alirón!
el Athletic es campeón.

Track 10

PARA ROMPER LA PIÑATA

Echen confites y canelones
pa' los muchachos
que son comilones.
Castaña asada, piña cubierta,
pa' los muchachos que van a la puerta.

Ándale, Lola,
no te dilates
con la canasta
de los cacahuates.

En esta posada
nos hemos chasqueado,
porque la dueña
nada nos ha dado.

Dale, dale, dale,
no pierdas el tino,
mide la distancia
que hay en el camino.

Track 11

LAS MAÑANITAS

Éstas son las mañanitas
que cantaba el Rey David,
pero no eran tan bonitas
como las cantan aquí.

[estribillo]
Despierta, mi bien, despierta,
mira que ya amaneció,
ya los pajarillos cantan,
la luna ya se metió.

Despierta, mi bien, despierta,
mira que ya amaneció,
ya los pajarillos cantan,
la luna ya se metió.

Si el sereno de la esquina
me quisiera hacer favor,
de apagar su linternita
mientras que pasa mi amor.

[estribillo]
Despierta, mi bien, despierta,
mira que ya amaneció,
ya los pajarillos cantan,
la luna ya se metió.

Despierta, mi bien, despierta,
mira que ya amaneció,
ya los pajarillos cantan,
la luna ya se metió.

Track 12

DE COLORES

De colores, de colores se visten los
campos en la primavera.
De colores, de colores son los pajaritos
que vienen de afuera.
De colores, de colores es el arco iris
que vemos salir.
Y por eso los grandes amores de
muchos colores me gustan a mí.
Y por eso los grandes amores de
muchos colores me gustan a mí.

De colores, de colores brillantes y finos
se viste la aurora.
De colores, de colores son los mil
reflejos que el sol atesora.
De colores, de colores se viste el
diamante que vemos lucir.
Y por eso los grandes amores de
muchos colores me gustan a mí.
Y por eso los grandes amores de
muchos colores me gustan a mí.

Track 13

QUIÉREME MUCHO

Quiéreme mucho, dulce amor mío,
que amante siempre te adoraré.
Yo con tus besos y tus caricias
mis sufrimientos acallaré.

Cuando se quiere de veras,
como te quiero yo a ti,
es imposible, mi cielo,
tan separados vivir.

Cuando se quiere de veras,
como te quiero yo a ti,
es imposible, mi cielo,
tan separados vivir,
tan separados vivir.

Es imposible, mi cielo,
tan separados vivir,
tan separados vivir, vivir.

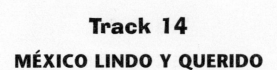

Track 14

MÉXICO LINDO Y QUERIDO

Voz de la guitarra mía,
al despertar la mañana,
quiere cantar su alegría
a mi tierra mexicana.

Yo le canto a tus volcanes,
a tus praderas y flores
que son como talismanes
del amor de mis amores.

México lindo y querido
si muero lejos de ti
que digan que estoy dormido
y que me traigan aquí.

México lindo y querido
si muero lejos de ti
que digan que estoy dormido
y que me traigan aquí.

Voz de la guitarra mía,
al despertar la mañana,
quiere cantar su alegría
a mi tierra mexicana.

Yo le canto a tus volcanes,
a tus praderas y flores
que son como talismanes
del amor de mis amores.

México lindo y querido
si muero lejos de ti
que digan que estoy dormido
y que me traigan aquí.

México lindo y querido
si muero lejos de ti
que digan que estoy dormido
y que me traigan aquí.

Track 15

MI CAFETAL

Porque la gente vive criticándome
Me paso la vida sin pensar en ná

Porque la gente vive criticándome
Paso la vida sin pensar en ná

Pero no sabiendo que yo soy el hombre
Que tengo un hermoso y lindo cafetal

Pero no sabiendo que yo soy el hombre
Que tengo un hermoso y lindo cafetal

Yo tengo mi cafetal
Y tú ya no tienes ná...

Yo tengo mi cafetal
Y tú ya no tienes ná...

Colombia mi tierra bonita

Nada me importa que la gente diga
Que no tengo plata que no tengo ná

Nada me importa que la gente diga
Que no tengo plata que no tengo ná

Pero no sabiendo que yo soy el hombre
Que tengo un hermoso y lindo cafetal

Pero no sabiendo que yo soy el hombre
Que tengo un hermoso y lindo cafetal

Yo tengo mi cafetal
Y tú ya no tienes ná..

Yo tengo mi cafetal
Y tú ya no tienes ná..

Track 16

MARÍA ISABEL

La playa estaba desierta,
el mar bañaba tu piel,
cantando con mi guitarra
para ti, María Isabel.

La playa estaba desierta,
el mar bañaba tu piel,
cantando con mi guitarra
para ti, María Isabel.

[estribillo]
Toma tu sombrero y póntelo,
vamos a la playa, calienta el sol.

Toma tu sombrero y póntelo,
vamos a la playa, calienta el sol.

Chiri biri bi, poro, pom, pom.
Chiri biri bi, poro, pom, pom.
Chiri biri bi, poro, pom, pom.
Chiri biri bi, poro, pom, pom.

En la arena escribí tu nombre
y luego yo lo borré
para que nadie pisara
tu nombre: María Isabel.

En la arena escribí tu nombre
y luego yo lo borré
para que nadie pisara
tu nombre: María Isabel.

[estribillo]
Toma tu sombrero y póntelo,
vamos a la playa, calienta el sol.

Toma tu sombrero y póntelo,
vamos a la playa, calienta el sol.

Chiri biri bi, poro, pom, pom.
Chiri biri bi, poro, pom, pom.
Chiri biri bi, poro, pom, pom.
Chiri biri bi, poro, pom, pom.

La luna fue caminando,
bajo las olas del mar;
tenía celos de tus ojos
y tu forma de mirar.

La luna fue caminando,
bajo las olas del mar;
tenía celos de tus ojos
y tu forma de mirar.

[estribillo]
Toma tu sombrero y póntelo,
vamos a la playa, calienta el sol.

Toma tu sombrero y póntelo,
vamos a la playa, calienta el sol.

Chiri biri bi, poro, pom, pom.
Chiri biri bi, poro, pom, pom.
Chiri biri bi, poro, pom, pom.
Chiri biri bi, poro, pom, pom.

Track 17

LA GOLONDRINA

A donde irá veloz y fatigada,
la golondrina que de aquí se irá,
allí en el cielo se mirará angustiada,
sin paz ni abrigo que dio mi amor.

Junto a mi pecho allí hará su nido,
En donde pueda la estacion pasar,
También yo estoy en la región perdida.
¡Oh cielo santo! Y sin poder volar.

También yo estoy en la región perdida.
¡Oh cielo santo! Y sin poder volar.

Junto a mi pecho allí hará su nido,
En donde pueda la estacion pasar,
También yo estoy en la región perdida.
¡Oh cielo santo! Y sin poder volar.

Track 18

¡VIVA JUJUY!

Vamos con ese bailecito

Adentrito cholo

¡Viva Jujuy!
¡Viva la Puna!
¡Viva mi amada!
¡Vivan los cerros
pintarrajeados
de mi quebrada...!

¡Viva Jujuy!
¡Viva la Puna!
¡Viva mi amada!
¡Vivan los cerros
pintarrajeados
de mi quebrada...!

De mi quebrada
humahuaqueña...

No te separes
de mis amores,
¡tú eres mi dueña!

La, lara, rara, rara

No te separes
de mis amores,
¡tú eres mi dueña!

Dos, dos y se va la otrita

Adentro

Viva Jujuy
y la hermosura
de las jujeñas!
Vivan las trenzas
bien renegridas
de mi morena!

Viva Jujuy
y la hermosura
de las jujeñas!
Vivan las trenzas
bien renegridas
de mi morena!

De mi morena
mal pagadora

No te separes
de mis amores
¡tú eres mi dueña!

La, lara, rara, rara

No te separes
de mis amores
¡tú eres mi dueña!

Track 19

ADIÓS MUCHACHOS

Adiós muchachos compañeros de mi vida,
barra querida, de aquellos tiempos.
Me toca a mí hoy emprender la retirada,
debo alejarme de mi buena muchachada.

Adiós, muchachos,
ya me voy y me resigno,
contra el destino nadie la talla.
Se terminaron para mí todas las farras.
Mi cuerpo enfermo no resiste más.

Dos lágrimas sinceras
derramo en mi partida
por la barra querida
que nunca me olvidó.
Y al darle a mis amigos
mi adiós postrero
les doy con toda el alma
mi bendición.

Adiós muchachos compañeros de mi vida,
barra querida, de aquellos tiempos.
Me toca a mí hoy emprender la retirada,
debo alejarme de mi buena muchachada.

Adiós, muchachos,
ya me voy y me resigno,
contra el destino nadie la talla.
Se terminaron para mí todas las farras.
Mi cuerpo enfermo no resiste más.